Upstate

Also by Jeremy Hooker:

Poetry
Landscape of the Daylight Moon
Soliloquies of a Chalk Giant
Solent Shore
Englishman's Road
A View from the Source
Master of the Leaping Figures
Their Silence a Language (with Lee Grandjean)
Our Lady of Europe
Adamah
Arnolds Wood
The Cut of the Light: Poems 1965-2005

Prose
Welsh Journal

Criticism
Poetry of Place
The Presence of the Past: Essays on Modern British and American Poetry
Writers in a Landscape
Imagining Wales: A View of Modern Welsh Writing in English

As editor:
Frances Bellerby: *Selected Stories*
Alun Lewis: *Selected Poems* (with Gweno Lewis)
At Home on Earth: A New Selection of the Later Writings of Richard Jefferies
Alun Lewis: *Inwards Where All the Battle Is: Writings from India*
Mapping Golgotha: A Selection of Wilfred Owen's Letters and Poems.
Edward Thomas: *The Ship of Swallows*

Jeremy Hooker

Upstate
A North American Journal

Shearsman Books
Exeter

Published in the United Kingdom in 2007 by
Shearsman Books Ltd
58 Velwell Road
Exeter EX4 4LD

ISBN-13   978-1-905700-22-6

ISBN-10   1-905700-22-9

Copyright © Jeremy Hooker, 2007

The right of Jeremy Hooker to be identified as the author of this work has been asserted by him in accordance with the Copyrights, Designs and Patents Act of 1988. All rights reserved. No part of this publication may be reproduced, stored in a retrieval system, transmitted in any form or by any means, electronic, mechanical, photocopying, recording or otherwise, without the prior permission of the publisher.

Acknowledgements
I wish to express my gratitude to Stephen Stuart-Smith at Enitharmon Press for permission to reprint the poems, 'Earth Song Cycle', 'Towards Arras', 'Hieratic Head of Ezra Pound', 'Vincent', 'Strata Florida (1)', 'Strata Florida (2)', and 'Imagining Wales' from my book, *Our Lady of Europe* (Enitharmon, 1997). An extract from *Upstate* appeared in *Scintilla* 8. My thanks to the editors, Anne Cluysenaar and Peter Thomas. The final shape of the book owes a great deal to my wife, Mieke, to whom I am deeply grateful.

The publisher gratefully acknowledges the financial assistance of
Arts Council England for its 2005-2007 publishing programme.

Upstate:
A North American Journal

For David Lloyd and Kim Waale

Preface

This journal is a record of a visit to North America with my wife, Mieke. During the academic year 1994-95 I was visiting professor at Le Moyne College near Syracuse in upstate New York. Our friends David Lloyd, the writer, and his wife, Kim Waale, the sculptor, were frequently our companions and guides in our explorations during the year. Through David and his family we were privileged to gain a special sense of areas settled by Welsh immigrants in upstate New York. This was our first, and so far, only, visit to America, and, for us, it was an experience of discovering places and a way of life that was new to us.

Of course, it is late in the day for anyone to imagine that they have 'discovered' America! In that sense of the word, there are few places in the world, if any, that remain undiscovered. Yet, for any mind that is alive the world is always new. However much we may gain from reading and study or benefit from other people's advice or experience, true knowledge is always first-hand.

This, no doubt, is one reason why some people keep diaries or journals. I looked recently for the first time into Julian Green's *Diary 1928-1957*, where, in the first entry, he writes: 'This diary . . . will help me, I think, to see more clearly into myself'. It would be futile to deny that keeping a journal involves a search for self-knowledge. But that was not what made me want to start a journal, when I was a student. Rather, it was a sense of wonder. I had been struck by the sight of some flowers – I think they were tulips – on a grassy bank in a street in Southampton, and I had been reading William Blake, a combined experience that impelled me to ask about the flowers' maker. Subsequent entries had more to do with self-recrimination over boozing and time wasting, and it was almost another ten years before, living in rural Wales, I began the writing that matters to me, which is essentially exploratory.

A few months later in his diary Julian Green, who has been reading Samuel Pepys, remarks that Pepys 'wrote for the pleasure of talking about himself. Now, I obey the incomprehensible desire to bring the past to a standstill that makes one keep a diary'. I can identify with this: the desire to capture the moment. This is impossible, of course, yet in the very attempt something of the life-sensation may be caught. The aim pertains also to memory, and may be valued especially by someone who has a poor memory for details, as I have. Simply making a note may be a poetic act, a humble attempt, in the words of Patrick Kavanagh in his poem 'The Hospital', to 'Snatch out of time the passionate transitory'.

I love the literary journal as a form, and delight in published diaries and notebooks – Dorothy Wordsworth, S. T. Coleridge, Francis Kilvert, H. D. Thoreau, these are among writers whose personal writings deserve to be known as bright books of life. What gives me special pleasure is the art of natural observation, which I first discovered as a boy in the essays of Richard Jefferies. It is an art which, at best, is not mere note taking or even picture-making, but involves an acute sensitivity to the life in things, to the quick of sentient existence. And the observation or perception is, in the kind of writing I have in mind, the origin of thinking. Jefferies's Notebooks reveal a man who never stopped thinking for himself, even when in great pain, to the end of his life. One could call this courage. One could say also that this was the man he was; there was no other way for him. And perhaps this is the way of Negative Capability, of the person who lives with doubts and uncertainties, and for whom the living detail is always the beginning of a fresh perception, a further adventure towards – where?

Keeping a journal is a means of seeing in the dark, and the dark always advances.

I have no interest in confession, although I am aware that my very selectivity – and every journal entry is a selection from countless possible impressions – is a form of self-revelation. My hope would be to speak in a way that opens upon common human depths. Self-consciousness, as I understand it, is less the material of a journal than a problem the person keeping a journal has to deal with, the more so once a possibility or intention of publication arises. It will be less of a problem, however, if one's aim is always to keep one's mind on the matter in hand, whether noting a natural effect, or engaging in a process of thought, or thinking about oneself. The one thing a diarist must never do is perform for an audience, even if the audience is only himself or herself. At best, I have found my journal a means of escaping from self-consciousness, since it is not about the ego in isolation, but about relationships between the seer and the seen, between self and other. If it is about finding oneself, it is about finding oneself in the world, neither of which is separable from the other.

It will be evident from the foregoing that I understand keeping a journal as analogous to writing poetry. It is not the same, but there are analogies. Each is about making a shape in words – a literary journal rarely consists of raw notations; its aim is to find the right word or image, to form the corresponding 'shape' for an impression or thought. In my case, too, the journal has sometimes served me as a 'quarry' of poetic materials, as well as a way of thinking about poetry.

Immediacy is a feature of journal entries, as it may also be of the poetic image – 'quickness' may characterize both. But it is not only the present moment in which one lives. *Upstate* is a journal in which I record impressions and ideas inspired by the day-to-day experience of living in upstate New York. Yet I was also during that period preoccupied with thinking about and imagining Europe, and writing poems that were subsequently published in my book, *Our Lady of Europe*. What North America gave me was experience of the New World. But it provided me also with the distance from which I could see the Old World in which I had lived. The contrast between 'new' and 'old' worlds enabled me to seek the terms in which each was most vividly alive.

29 August 1994
In the air at last, cloud below us and land under cloud-shadow visible below the clouds, sunlight shining on the edge of the wing. We left Frome this morning after several days of frantic preparations. When Mieke & I visited my father in the nursing home, he said, over & over again, 'Never mind, Jeremy' & 'No one stands for me' – by which, reverting to his early days, he meant no one supports him. As I write this, I can see Portland joined to the land by a narrow strip, the long shingle beach of Chesil, far below. And now we are following the coast: small, irregular green & brown fields with cloud puffs above them, visible through a darkish gauzy light.

Turbulent now – pen shaking too much to write.

Small white clouds like gunsmoke. Land & islands like pieces of jigsaw, sea dimpled & shimmering.

At 35,000 feet with a floor of woolly cloud below us & below that the Atlantic. And here we are cramped in our seats looking at tiny screens set into the seat backs in front showing silly films, only five hundred years after the tiny boats crossed the 'green sea of darkness' & the conquest & white colonization of the New World began.

How this would have startled Brendan & the early voyagers. Would they have found the world full of miracles if they could have travelled in air-conditioned comfort above it? Even to us, who seldom travel by air, the experience is less than marvellous. Yet the achievement is amazing when one considers the beginnings of flight, let alone the time before, when for ages flight was a wonderful dream. How quickly though we have got used to our own technological new world and taken for granted what would have seemed miracles even to our Victorian ancestors.

As I look out of the window along the wing I see a kind of sublime vacancy. Above, the blue dome of the sky; below, the cloud-floor shaped like wind-moulded drifts of snow, but insubstantial, because the blue sky appears through rifts & open spaces. As it becomes more broken, the cloud might be ice floes on a sky-blue sea. It is beautiful, and vast, and in relation to the oceanic cloud we seem to be moving very slowly. For some reason, I think of the Soviet astronaut who believed he had categorically disproved the existence of God, because he found no sign of God in space. It's easy to laugh but in fact most of us are drunk on the ideas our age lives by, its faith that there's nothing anywhere except man & his concepts & images.

For a long time we have been flying above continuous flat cloud but now, though the cloud is still continuous, it forms an extraordinary hilly landscape, all stacks & whirls & twisted upthrust formations, like the surface of a strange planet.

39,000 feet over the Gulf of St Lawrence. All blue under us, a great depth of blue.

Over the coast, a distinct orangey-red line. Fields, roads, houses, a relief map with raised patches of trees. Again the smaller clouds & cloud-shadows under them, dark shapes, like jelly fish, drawn across the surface of the land.

Coming in over the water at Boston, another jet below us, small as a toy.

Three hours later. A dark, clear night, patterns of lights on the ground & the after-sunset glow to our right. On the way to Syracuse.

2 September
We have come to an area of pinewoods & low hills – a drumlin landscape; prosperous suburban America, but spacious, with a remote feel of the early continent, a just perceptible sense of the wild land, around secluded & well-protected residences. Our landlady, Terrie Sopher, insists on calling our roomy & beautifully appointed apartment a 'suite'. It is above hers, in a wooden building she herself designed. She has it well secured with a system of locks & alarms which makes me feel jumpy, because I don't yet understand it. She too makes me feel nervous; she's intelligent & well meaning & very helpful towards us, but this is very much *her* house, and I'm afraid of doing something careless, like forgetting to lock a door or setting off an alarm. Terrie's late husband was professor of geography at Syracuse University – it was an eerie experience for me to look at the bookshelves in our suite and find books on landscape & place . . .

The people we've met have been enormously welcoming – David & Kim who met us at the airport when we arrived, and colleagues, Barron & Pat, with whom we had a meal & drank a lot of delicious South African red wine the evening after our arrival. But also many other people in the college, which has a relaxed, friendly atmosphere.

The welcome has given us great pleasure and its immediacy is part of the *difference* of being here, but doesn't altogether account for it. There are things that seem superficially different – cars, road systems, architecture, wealth of goods in the stores. And everywhere the different peoples, almost all of them Americans, who belong here, as we do not. I don't want to start with false ideals, and I'm aware of a crassness that almost beggars belief. But I already have a sense of a much larger degree of democracy than I'm used to in England with its little dictatorships, snobberies, & resentful assumptions of inferiority.

And there's the space, as I was told there would be. Here the space immediately around us, which isn't much different from that in a well-to-do, leafy English suburb, but also, with a feeling of a remnant of original wilderness among trees & 'small lawns of home', openings towards far-off horizons – the Great Lakes, the Adirondacks, the Catskills, all the country to New York City & the coast.

There's no doubt that what we've come to – despite deer & squirrels in the pinewoods around – is a life of great luxury, the greatest, in terms of distribution, the world has ever known. And this too gives a different feel to things. Not wholly a welcome one, in the measures taken to protect it, for example, & in the obsession with bodily well being & with securing the personal – *me*, *my* things, *my* place – against intrusion, that goes with it. But it would be merely hypocritical for me to deny the benefit of conveniences & facilities, & my pleasure in the goods on display.

A call from Joe in France, where he & Maddy went with the lorry to travel and earn some money a few days before we left England. He wanted to know how M. and I would feel about being grandparents! Even seemed a little doubtful we would be pleased! And of course we're delighted to know that Maddy is two-months pregnant and they intend to have the child. Afterwards M. cried. And I could see so clearly the little boy I used to walk with in the fields round Brynbeidog, and take to and fetch from school.

A grey squirrel chak-chakked from a vertical pine branch outside the window this morning and its plume of a tail stood up waving violently.

I couldn't see what was agitating it. Later we drove downtown to the Federal Building to set in motion the process that will get me a social security number. I feel already that America will offer me, as it has countless others, an opportunity of freedom – a loosening of creative restrictions maybe – although I'm not sure what form it will take.

4 September
Sunday morning excursion, with Terrie driving, to Skaneateles (by one of the Finger Lakes) for brunch in a restaurant. Afterwards, with several wrong turnings, we drove to Beaver Lake. Woods, vibrant with cicadas, surrounding a lake of green-brown water. An area of marked & illustrated trails, like the New Forest, only more so, with a joky information board every few yards: Nature as mass entertainment. 'Swamplands are the supermarkets of the wild, producing an abundant food supply for animals and fish . . .' 'All around you a great factory is at work' (picture of the interior of a leaf as a factory), juxtaposed with ' the miracle of green and growing things'. Until 1960 the lake was called Mud Lake, which may have been a translation of the Indian name. One picture by the lakeside showed a red man looking out across the water. Returning from a day's hunting he relaxes, enjoying the scene, as we also may relax . . . I feel closer to nature watching the black-capped chickadees (as I've learnt to call them) flitting about in the hawthorn with big red berries which leans over our verandah and coming to drink at the water-bowl.

5 September
Labor Day. I spent most of the time preparing classes until the late afternoon of another warm, sunny day, when we walked along the road and into St Mary's Catholic cemetery, which occupies a large hilly area (bigger than most English city parks) between here and Le Moyne College. We saw our first raccoon by the roadside – a dead one, lying on its back – and, in the cemetery, our first groundhog, so absorbed with head down in grass beside the path that for a time it didn't see us. I was struck by the newness of the smooth grey stones, most with Irish names: none worn out or indistinct and no stone sunken or fallen apart, as in our English graveyards with their invitations to easy reverie. This is indeed a city of the dead. A few maples among the stones are beginning to flame.

6 September
At the end of my first full day's work I was exhausted. The Shakespeare class is large – 33 students – and will be hard to animate. The creative writing class has half that number, and the students are committed. The modern British novel class is a little smaller. Not much participation yet, except among the writers, so I talk too much, try too hard to make things happen. And then, when someone does speak, I often don't hear properly! At the end of the day my head was dully singing.

7 September
Tired last night, and feeling the difficulties of being here – How far will our money go? Will we be able to afford a car? To travel? Will we adapt to the constrictions of the suite? – and thinking about our home & life in England – I doubted that we had done the right thing in coming here. But this morning everyone in college was immediately so helpful, my spirits rose. I felt reassured, glad to be here.

For the time being, as far as my work goes, I have left something complete behind me. Now's the time to move on, to gain new experiences: to renew my sense of imaginative possibility. I like the expansive American gesture – it's what appeals to me in the poetry – Whitman, Charles Olson – in the spaces of the land, but also in the friendly openness of the people. Sometimes it's superficial, but not always, and I don't automatically assume it is. What I want anyway is to go beneath the surface.

Evening At Barnes and Noble listening to David reading poems by Gillian Clarke from his new book, *The Urgency of Identity: Contemporary English-Language Poetry from Wales*, to a small audience. Strange to stand in the bookstore and think of her 'small cottage near Lampeter', as David called Blaen Cwrt.

Pat Keane read an extract from his new book, *Coleridge's Submerged Politics*. Afterwards we went with him, Barron, David & Kim, & Jonathan, a philosopher who had read from his book on criminal law, to a bar and drank several jugs of beer. They are so friendly towards us, and good humoured with each other, that we at once feel included. But I feel rather shy, too, and afraid of being too ponderous, as I always do in the company of quick-witted people.

8 September
A better teaching day with a more fluent rhythm. The large Shakespeare class is going to be difficult – so little response so far that I haven't the faintest idea what they really think of the play, or make of what I'm saying, or of me! They sit quite still, looking at me, sometimes taking notes, reading parts, with little expression, when I ask them to. And I stand in front of them or walk up and down, getting excited with ideas or throwing myself into reading, with no idea of what they make of any of it.

The other classes, especially the creative writing workshop, are coming alive, which makes teaching so much easier & more enjoyable!

And occasionally I get to sit in my office, and look out of the window over college buildings and the campus onto a great plain. This looks more natural than suburban but in fact is rather the latter, with groups of houses among trees. In the near distance, airplanes periodically fly in low and disappear from sight, landing at the airport. Far off, the vague outline of a mountain range – the Adirondacks, I think.

Most of the houses we pass near the college, standing apart from each other in comfortable suburbs, are made of clapperboard.

9 September
Thunder & lightning, at times almost overhead, woke me in the night and I lay in bed reading Pat Keane's Introduction to his book. This immediately impressed me by its engagement with contemporary intellectual issues. Pat manoeuvres intelligently in a tricky & even desperate situation – in effect, a mental war fought by extremists on Left and Right – and in my view uses what is most valuable in radical historicism while retaining a firm grasp on aesthetic values. I was all too aware of academic *hatred* from my own experience, but he brings home to me the extent & ferocity of the warfare – not guns, but words & ideas, which kill the soul – between ideological positions and on grounds of ethnic, gender, and cultural differences. One of the main issues, as I was already aware, was the guilty hatred of Western civilization that has arisen in recent years among white middle-class intellectuals. There is in this a powerfully insidious mixture of justified anger – at slavery, exploitation, patriarchal attitudes, and so on – puritanical self-hatred & ideologically narrow readings of the evidence. What so few of us can

stand are mixed feelings, and a cultural heritage that produces them, and virtually *embeds* us in the ambiguities of love-and-hate, good-and-evil, right-and-wrong. It isn't that I think we should wallow in these, refuse to reason, fail to discriminate between right and wrong. What I feel rather is that with 'pure' mind we dehumanize ourselves.

We need to recognize past evils while acknowledging our links with both victims and perpetrators. (How shall I know my humanity if I can't imagine the suffering and outrage of the former, but also the capacity for inflicting injury that I share with the latter?) What's more difficult, though, is to recognize *present* evils – the forms of moral blindness, injustice, and cruelty to which we in our time are prone. In my small if vociferous world, which is mainly literary & academic, the evil I know is that of the Manichean mind, the ideologically 'pure' with its interrogation of *all* mysterious presence, whether in person or poem.

I don't want to stand for muddle or confusion; I want to see more clearly & more variously. But I want also to be able to admire, and love, and feel awe. I do in any case feel these things, and they mean admitting mixed feelings. Seeing the things of which I'm made doesn't only mean seeing *through* them.

> '*The United States themselves are essentially the greatest poem.*'
> Walt Whitman

Syracuse, the city close to which we will be living for nine months, is in Onondaga County. The Onondagas belonged to the Confederacy of the Five Nations, and were situated between the Mohawk Nation, 'Keeper of the Eastern Door', and the Senecas, 'Keeper of the Western Door'.

The red men were the first to slash and burn the forest to clear the fields. The women were the farmers. They planted many varieties of beans and squash between rows of corn. They called these 'our supporters' and revered the spirit-sisters that guarded them.

During the Revolution soldiers with 'a good eye for country' tramped over New York interior, destroying Indian food supplies. 'No doubt more than one soldier who set fire to a cornfield decided that he was burning a better crop than he had ever seen at home and resolved to come back after the war and claim a piece of such land for his own.'

The New Military Tract: 150,000 acres in Oneida-Onondaga districts were designated to soldiers (600 – 6,000 acres each, depending on rank).

Most major roads follow Indian trails in New York State. Genesee Street – New York's Route 5 – replaced an Indian trail, 'deepened with the steady tread of moccasins'.

The Iroquois acted as middlemen in the trade between the English and Dutch on one hand, and the Indians of the interior on the other. 'Competition between Hurons and Iroquois for the Great Lakes area customers who wanted European artifacts shaped the destiny of a continent and gave New York its outline for emergence.'

> *Syracuse, once South Salina: a short distance from the salt works at a point near where a north branch of the Genesee Street crossed Onondaga Creek. The salt springs along Onondaga Lake, in swampy country notorious for summer fevers, were a focus of activity from the earliest days of colonization. Lowering the level of Onondaga Lake in 1822 drained the swamp.*[1]

> *This confederacy consisted of the Senecas, Oneidas, Onondagas, Cayugas, Mohawks, and Tuskaroras; and until the innovations of white people, with their destructive engines of war – with whiskey and small-pox, they held their sway in the country, carrying victory, and consequently terror and dismay, wherever they warred. . . . Their combined strength, however, in all its might, poor fellows, was not enough to withstand the siege of their insidious foes . . .*
> George Catlin, North American Indians (1844)

13 September

My feelings towards the new are ambivalent. On one hand I enjoy its familiarities, and recognize that without them democracy – the relative freedom & livelihoods of millions of people – could not be sustained. ('Primitivist' thinking, to which I'm strongly attracted, caters for an intellectual minority: I'm not aware that it could do anything for the mass of Americans, except abandon them.) On the other hand I see the superficiality of our prevailing civilization, which, with the power of its

---

[1] Information and quotations drawn from D.W. Meining, in John H. Thompson (ed.), *Geography of New York State*.

images, is the most insidious that ever has existed, producing a mental world that seems all encompassing, killing our sense of nature (as our poisons kill Nature herself) and seemingly making it impossible for us to see or imagine differently.

The very spirit of poetry breathes hopelessness in this air. A condition that doesn't *necessarily* produce hopeless poetry, while the characteristic freshness of American poetry relates subtly to revolutionary hope: the hope of making a new beginning, of radical change, and (in Whitman and William Carlos Williams for example) of revolutionizing poetry itself, and replacing European models with a poetry that voices *this* land and *this* people.

No wonder Ivor Gurney was attracted to Whitman, and Richard Jefferies fell under the spell of *Leaves of Grass*. I too have long felt the attraction – and while I dislike Whitman's rhetoric, turning to his poetry has always been to me like opening doors and windows when I feel suffocated by my own culture, or unable to write a line of poetry that breathes.

But I know we are far from his day, and from what felt like its renewal, in the 1960s. Not far in actual years, but in mental time, inside the suffocating sphere of our image-world. Yet I don't feel hopeless. I'm curious; I want to see and to understand. The days when it was possible to explore the continent are over, but experience is always new, and all true poetic life is exploration.

16 September
Morning. A pair of white-breasted nuthatches among the Scots pines, running up and down the trunks, and spiralling round them, pecking insects from the bark. The other bird unfamiliar to me, which haunts the garden, is the blue jay. So far I've only glimpsed it, but we often hear its harsh cry. When I was a boy, at school at Rope Hill, Mr Randall, the English teacher, who first woke my interest in *modern* poetry, showed us one of his own poems, in which he mentioned a blue jay. And I criticized the image, on the grounds that our jay wasn't the blue jay!

> *A history of the United States must be a history of victors; the defeated are relevant chiefly for what they tell us of their conquerors.*
> Hugh Brogan, *The Penguin History of the United States of America*

Why? The victors' fascination with the conquered (the redskins) tells us something about their guilty consciences (the consciences of sensitive descendants who haven't had to struggle for a place to live in), but probably even more about the loss or destruction of a sense of the sacred. For to the Native Americans this land was sacred ground. With the death of the sacred we are dying spiritually, and Nature (Mother of the Wild Things) may die indeed.

So we turn to the wisdom of the aboriginal people, as we should. But we cannot thereby *become* them without denying their identity, and betraying our own. We can become wiser by getting outside our own skins, but we can't abandon them. It isn't merely 'balance' or fair-mindedness I want. What I want is the truth that lies in meeting; but also understanding of what one is by virtue of western civilization, with its religious inheritance, and meeting with native wisdom, which our ancestors overrode.

For all its limitations born of racial prejudice, there's an honesty about the ambivalence & even the confusion of *Heart of Darkness* that is lacking in the primitivism of the colonialists' heirs, and in our politically correct retrospection. The 'message' may be profoundly pessimistic: the West is hollow at the core, resting on an idealism that is an illusion. But Joseph Conrad recognized himself as a beneficiary of the 'light' won from the 'darkness' that once enveloped the site of London, as a result of 'robbery with violence, aggravated murder on a great scale, and men going at it blind'.

I write, not to condone crimes against humanity, but with a sense that, *now,* one of our most insidious temptations is an impossible 'purity', a righteousness of thought, which denies the mixed people most of us are. To say that without slavery there would have been no black America isn't to condone slavery; nor does it justify the conquest of the Indians to say that there would have been no white America without it. What is justice to the mind of God, or in the scale of human history? How could any mortal know? We have ourselves to seek to be just in the circumstances of our times. It's my sense of justice that, for better or worse, often makes me take up a position neither on one side or the other, but *between*. It's there, where different things come together, that I find the greatest sense of human possibility.

Evening
David drove us to Cazenovia, where we met Kim and visited the college at which she teaches. The small town – David calls it a village – is one of the oldest in the State. It was founded in the late 18th century, close to a beautiful lake, which, unlike Onondaga Lake, isn't polluted. The college, with older stone buildings and graceful buildings of red brick, stands on the site of the first Madison County Court House. A student band was playing Latin American music on a college lawn, as we walked round, and along streets shaded by tall maples. After dark, a gibbous moon, appearing & disappearing among cloud, but clear & bright later, after we had had a meal in a restaurant and walked to the lake.

The thing most to be avoided, always, is playing God: reconciling the irreconcilable in the mind.

17 September
Terrie took us to Founders' Day dinner at Syracuse University, where we mixed with alumni and students in the lobby of the Geology Building. Halfway through our meal, which we were eating at one of the round tables set out in the lobby, members of the SU football team, with mascot & female cheerleaders, came into the room, and paraded round chanting their war chant. We were among the very few who didn't go to the game afterwards, and we walked back to the car against a crowd streaming towards the Dome. The function of the students at the dinner – confident, personable young men & women – is to mix with the old people – the alumni – and talk about the university past and present. I was able to slip away for a minute and look at the fossil dinosaurs – a Pliosaurus, a Plesiosaurus, and an Ichthyosaurus – exhibited on the wall: one had been found near Dorchester, the other two at Glastonbury, in England.

18 September
A Sunday afternoon drive with Terrie to where she & her husband used to live, in a house in the hills above Oneida Lake, which we glimpsed below us, in blue light under broken masses of cloud. Afterwards we drove to Chittenango, and walked a short distance along the old Erie Canal – in its day (built 1817-1825) the great channel for trade, which ran from Lake Erie to the Hudson. Today, a few leaves were drifting on the

surface of grey-green water. From there to Chittenango Falls, where the creek drops 167 feet into a gorge cut through limestone. We stood above it, where the water flows between boulders which it has washed smooth &, literally, streamlined, before falling into the gorge. Before driving to Cazenovia, where we had tea in the gracious surroundings of an old restaurant – alone in a high-ceilinged room, we helped ourselves to tea from silver teapots set out on a table at the farther end – we visited Stone Quarry Hill, where there is an art gallery & a sculpture park. Here we walked in the beautiful garden – partly cultivated, partly left wild – in warm sunlight, and looked down at other hills. It was beautiful, and reminded me of Welsh hill country, &, perhaps for that reason, I felt a little empty, because I have no associations with this country – its 'white' history, which I scarcely know, is so recent, its 'aboriginal' history so vast. Yet I am drawn to it, too, and as we drove among the hills, occasionally glimpsing Oneida Lake below, and approaching Syracuse again, I sensed a little more of the patterns of the land.

20 September
A cloudless day. I lectured on *Twelfth Night* in the morning and on *Howards End* in the afternoon. In between, a writing workshop – the Ruskin exercise, listening to what the students had *seen*. So many things, each one different.

21 September
Another day without a cloud in the sky.
    Sitting on the verandah in the shade of the Scots pine & the hawthorn, which has dropped big red berries on the planks under my feet. A light breeze stirring the leaves & occasional quick nervous movements of chickadees. With the sound of cicadas, more constant than the louder noise of construction noise nearby, & the resinous smell & beautiful flaky bark of the pines, the place reminds me of the chalet we stayed in in Spain.
    In life & death we are all completely wrapped up in the unknown. Genetic inheritance can't explain the wonder of individual consciousness, the birth of awareness we don't question, because we know nothing else. So we appear, and the world appears with us, and eventually we disappear, and the world we know disappears from us. I

don't begin to understand what it means, however much I read about evolution & the creation of the universe. I don't say we can know nothing, only that in the matters that concern us most – consciousness and death – we are wrapped in darkness. And the only wisdom I know is to love it, all of it, including death, which we will share with those we love. I can't imagine the world *not*, I can never come close to imagining nothing. And perhaps it isn't for us to do so, because we have no business with 'it'. But say no thing, which is beyond our capacity to conceive or imagine, and may be the ground of all that is . . .

The breeze is a little stronger now; I can feel it moving my shirt against my skin. Now & then a leaf or a pine needle falls, a small bird chirps, and though the clouds I can see are small, there is a perceptible diminution of the warmth & brightness of the sun. That steady sound of the cicadas, we hear it all day and we hear it when we wake up in the night. One could imagine it the sound of the machinery of life itself. Only soon it will be still, in the long cold winter everyone tells us is to come.

> *'As to me I know of nothing else but miracles . . .'*
> Walt Whitman

25 September

A Sunday morning drive and walk round Green Lake. This is one of two glacial lakes in the park. The meronictic lakes, with surface & bottom waters that never mix, were formed in the plunge basin of a waterfall, and are very deep. The water is turquoise, and now reflects the colours of the autumnal woods that surround it, growing on hillsides rising steeply from its banks. Conifers grow on the very edge and many, stripped of bark, have fallen in, and lie like ghastly skeletons under the water, or stick out like the 'sword' of some prehistoric beast. Tangled limbs under water, knotty root systems, contorted pale torsos, and rotted trunks already half mingled with the earth. The water seemed still until we looked, and saw ripples, leaves floating on the surface, a fallen insect spinning round and round. And the woods seemed quiet until we heard the cicadas, the cry of a jay, a bird or insect making a noise like a telephone ringing in a farther room, an airplane's drone.

Other couples were walking round the lake, and parents with young children, and now and then a jogger trotted past. Most people we met said hello or hi cheerfully. Faint but warm & sweet, the woods were beginning to exude a smell of decay.

For some reason – perhaps the sense of mysterious depth – I thought of the first still water I fished in, the lake at Newlands Manor near Milford, which was to me most wonderful, a magical place. I would usually go with a friend, and we would leave our bikes in the hedge, near the road bridge, which was said to be haunted by the ghost of a poor boy who had lived close by and, together with his whole family, died of diphtheria. The bridge was known after him as Cox's Bridge.

Newlands Manor lake was full of small rudd, but while we were catching them, big golden carp would hurl themselves out of the water and fall back in with a mighty splash. I have never seen carp fling themselves into the air as often as those fish did.

The days of magic & expectation were short lived. They came to an end one day when I was wading in the lake with bare legs, struck at a bite and hooked a small rudd clean out of the water, accidentally swinging it with a smack into my friend Roger's face. We must have been making a lot of noise because when we turned to the bank three men in dark suits were standing there watching us. One of them told us off for abusing the freedom of the lake and ordered us to leave.

I found my way to other lakes and ponds afterwards, but none of them had quite the magic of Newlands Manor lake, with the abandon of big golden carp leaping out and falling back.

The water (for me, the primary source of inspiration, and very element of reminiscence), the lovely aquamarine water, with its slightly menacing look, made me think and talk about the past.

I loved the places to which I belonged as a boy, and to which, for some time afterwards, unselfconsciously, I felt I still belonged. And that original feeling has shaped all my relationships to the world. Not always wisely or for the better (I sometimes see myself as a big overfriendly dog eager to jump up and lick everyone on the face, or anxious to propitiate dogs of a different temper), but it is what I have, nevertheless, to work with.

Happiness can stupefy with self-absorption. It's also necessary to imagine differently; to see the world as it appears to others, even as ugly, violent, dark. To the other who is other, but also to the other who is an aspect or potential of oneself. I would like to write a book that is true to my happy self. But I would like also to get out of my skin, and to extend my imaginative sympathy.

1 October

> *Whites brought the idea of the 'savage' to this continent. Huron, from the French, 'wild boar'. Iroquois, from Hilokoa (Basque for 'Killer People'). Iroquois called themselves Hodenosaunee, 'People of the Longhouse'.*
>
> *Onondaga: 'People of the Hills'. Keepers of the Central Fire in the Longhouse.*

A drive in rain to the south of Syracuse. Pompey – Fabius – Apulia – Tully. Through hill country, mist smoking from wooded slopes. Colours of fall leaves damply smouldering. Country of scattered farms, most of them made of wood. Ramshackle wooden barns painted red or brown. Sometimes the farmhouses, too, look neglected. There may have been other buildings on the same site earlier. The 'new' look of habitations in this country is due in part to the fact that aging buildings are pulled down and replaced. Here and there a small graveyard, tombstones in a circle of trees, more populous than the land for miles around appears to be.

It's the emotion in a dream that impresses an image on the mind, when most vanish without leaving a touch. Fear, as I crouch over the handlebars of a big motorbike, with my brother Dave on the pillion, and ride down Ramley Road and past the Common. Sacred awe, as I handle ancient objects (one like a headless Christ shaped in the form of a mother-goddess) unearthed from an old building, where I am working with Lindsay Clarke.

Waking, I recognize one formative influence on the latter. We had talked with the poets Barbara Clarkson[2] and her partner Jack about the historical 'depth' of English landscapes, compared to the newness of America. Barbara had felt it acutely when she visited England, and found

---

[2] Barbara published her poetry under the name Barbara Moore. Her books are: *Farewell to the Body* (The Word Works, 1990), and *The Flame Tree* (BASFAL Books, 1996).

it awe-inspiring, although she appreciated that it could be suffocating, too.

Dave would have been 67 tomorrow. I find it hard to realize he is dead.

2 October
At Round Lake, cupped among woods that descend steeply to its sides. Wind silvering the surface. Leaves & raindrops making circles in calm water near the shore. Now the smell of decay from the woods is stronger, sweeter, and leaves fall in flurries. Hoof-shaped bracket fungi clustered on a fallen rotting tree trunk. They look as if they are clamped on, sucking the life out of the wood – in fact breaking it down, releasing elements & minerals for re-use.

We stand in sunlight at the water's edge and I dip my fingers in, finding it still quite warm in the shallows. The woods on the side of the lake below the sun are in shadow, the woods on the other side are dark red, orange, yellow, rust among many shades of green. The water mirrors the colours. Boulders lie scattered here & there on the hillsides & by the lake – erratics, which rode here on the ice. It's possible to imagine water falling from a great height. As the wooded hills drop to the lake so we can envisage the floor of the lake falling down & down. Tentacular roots & branches submerged at the margin plunge into aquamarine depths.

All is alive, the lake, the woods, the sun, the clouds blowing over. The Earth is alive (Gaia): the great organic system & the manifold small systems that are part of it. We were told about the Spirit that brooded on the face of the waters. Once people lived here who believed there was a spirit in everything. They were right; it's a truer story than the story of dead matter. I'm tempted to think of the lake as a mind (and the mind as still, deep water), but draw back, aware of the danger of anthropomorphism. I feel it to be a great being, utterly strange to me, in a world full of beings – trees birds fungi squirrels insects ourselves among them. I know we are all one, all of the same substance. But I can't resign the wonder of consciousness, by which I perceive the oneness. What I see is the unique centre of every being – the uniqueness I know in myself and other humans. What it is to each & every one in the rest of nature, I don't know. But it exists, nature is full of beings, countless & strange to us, as eyes of sunlight on the water.

7 October

An October day which might have been made in paradise. I walked among the woods at the edge of the cemetery and lay down on the grass in the sun. Tall slender maples with scales of grey bark, leaves shaking & rustling, leaves spinning down, an airplane high up, twin vapour trails crossing blue sky seen through branches. Crows cawing, one perched on a tombstone. A pair of yellow butterflies fluttering round & round each other, rising, for all the world as if it were spring.

8 October

Today we set out to drive to the Adirondacks. At Oriskany battlefield on another perfect day. The monument, a tall obelisk, constructed from stones of the dismantled Erie Canal, commemorates the battle fought between Loyalists and Revolutionary troops, in driving rain, on 6 August 1777. There were Indians on both sides, and, for the British, Joseph Brant, with 400 Mohawk & Seneca supported Sir John Johnson and 50 Royal Greens. The Revolutionary leader, General Herkimer, was killed in the battle, which the monument presents as a victory for his forces: 'The British Invasion was checked and thwarted'. It commemorates Herkimer & his men: 'The lifeblood of more than two hundred Patriot heroes made this battleground Sacred Forever'. Brant & his men & the other Loyalists are only mentioned – this in 1877, when the monument was erected – as the enemy. It would be hard to imagine a more peaceful site than this is today, on a hillside above the wooded Mohawk valley – hickory, maple, dark red sumac – with a distant view of Adirondack foothills. One bronze on the side of the monument shows Herkimer, wounded, directing the battle. Another shows a musket man bayoneting a red man with tomahawk raised to strike. Why doesn't the monument commemorate *all* who fell in the battle? Today it would probably have to. Were the wounds still raw in 1877, or is it really a symbol of white supremacy?

In the Adirondacks we took a slow journey on a tourist train through the woods, glimpsing rapids on the Moose River, a beaver lodge on a pond. Boulders among grey tree trunks, a trickle of falling leaves. Monarch butterflies, which seemed as big as small birds, fluttered round the station. Some fell by the wayside – those that won't make the journey to Mexico.

We spent the night in a cabin by a lake at Inlet.

9 October

At the Adirondack Museum at Blue Mountain Lake. Huge head of a moose on the wall, presiding over exhibits of kayaks, canoes & other watercraft. 'I could fall in love with a boat' (Mieke). The view of the lake below was awe-inspiring: conifer islands in water darkened & roughened by wind, blue mountains in cloud at the back, wooded lower down, wind suddenly blowing leaves up from the trees below us, swirling high overhead & falling down. Everywhere among the mountains the trees burned red & yellow; even brighter against grey, dead trees or trees that have already shed their leaves, smoky grey, grey of old man's beard.

It was raining when, in late afternoon, we stayed at a motel close to Whiteface Mountain and the Ausable River falls.

10 October

In the morning we walked by the falls & among the trees, coming upon one of the many pools of black swamp water with dead, white birches sticking up.

Lake Placid among the High Peaks. How to describe the commerce, the communion of mountains & clouds? The mountains seem to rise towards the clouds (as they do, at three millimetres per year!), sun brightening, cloud-shadow darkening, trees of red & yellow flame

We went to Bolton Landing to pay our respects to the memory of the sculptor, David Smith, who had lived and worked there. We might have seen his home from behind a fence but chose not to. Nothing else of his remains there. All the sculptures 'wound up in museums,' we were informed.

Back to Syracuse via Saratoga Springs & Utica. Flags flying outside homes for Columbus Day, Halloween pumpkin heads & masks & witches on porches.

I came back feeling ill with a sore throat, which jaundiced my view. Tom Dilworth wrote to me recently that when he visited the Adirondacks he kept wanting to compare them to Wales, but couldn't. I felt the same. The difference is between a cultural landscape, rich with a people's history & celebrated in their poetry, story & song, and a landscape – some of it wilderness – only recently opened up, with settlements based largely on the tourist industry & a good deal of temporary accommodation. The mountains don't belong to us, or we to them, though we have littered their fringes with our trashy civilization.

18 October

First day back at work after several days in bed feeling ill and weak. Mother died two years ago today. I have been thinking about her a lot recently, wishing we could talk.

19 October

I still feel weak and have little interest in food. A curious feature of this illness is that it has given me – and M. too, who's now suffering from the same virus – a reaction against being here. Partly it's a reaction against American food! But it's more than that, something affecting my whole system, like a physical distaste: nausea at a way of life. Watching TV doesn't help! A constant bright superficial chattering about money food & cars, hysteria & sentimentality, sentimentality & hysteria. A lot of moving about over the surface, where even nature's colours seem painted on. It's an odd sensation, no doubt due to my weakness, but I feel that I can't get my feet down to the ground, or as if there's nothing there to stand on, under the tarmac, only this superficial crust . . .

This certainly wasn't how I felt before we set out for the Adirondacks, when I walked in lovely October sunlight in & around the woods by the cemetery, or when we visited Green Lake and Round Lake. But somehow, as we drove up into the mountains . . .

But I was already beginning to feel ill then, and when we came down to Bolton Landing and instead of finding work by David Smith, even a single piece to show where he had lived and worked, we went into an 'Indian' store, a white store selling a trash of pseudo-Indian crafts & gee gaws . . .

And there's a lot of that in America, it's no good closing one's eyes to it, it has to be seen, along with the good things. It isn't that there's no past, far from it; there are lies about the past, and of course we too have those, in England, & maybe it's the nature of every civilized society to tell lies about the past, & none of us could live with the truth. But here there seems to be a widespread refusal to get in touch with the actual earth, in the sense of the movements of peoples shaping it. There's an idealized whiteness, & an idealized blackness, looking to Africa instead of America . . . It's hard to say what I mean, because I'm interpreting a feeling, and I don't know enough. There's something in the American experience, in its democratic impulses & bringing together of peoples, that I deeply respect. Even the superficial isn't to be scorned automatically; there's no superior position – some solider English ground – from which I can judge what I see. All I must do is be true to feelings, including ill feelings.

> *As the Incas conceived of Four Quarters radiating from Cusco to the rim of the world, the Iroquois pictured a Tree of Peace rising heavenward from the Longhouse, its four great roots reaching to the corners of the earth . . .*
> *Onondaga Lake . . . is today hemmed in by a freeway, a fairground, and the bungaloid growth of Syracuse. Somewhere beneath concrete and asphalt lies the spot where the Peacemaker, a divine hero, alighted from a white stone canoe and expounded his Great Law to the warring Iroquois.*
> Ronald Wright, *Stolen Continents*

(Note: 'bungaloid': how easily liberal sentiments become, in their turn, vicious and the noble dead are used as an excuse for scorning the living: all those unpicturesque people, blue collar workers, in their bungalows.)

> *The white man does not understand the Indian for the reason that he does not understand America. He is too far removed from its formative processes. The roots of the tree of his life have not yet grasped the rock and soil. The white man is still troubled with primitive fears . . . The man from Europe is still a foreigner and an alien. And he still hates the man who questioned his path across the continent.*
> Luther Standing Bear, Lakota Sioux, 1933

> *Wherever Christians have passed, conquering and discovering, it seems as though a fire has gone, consuming everything.*
> Pedro de Cieza de Leon, c. 1550
> Both quoted in Wright

24 October
Writing again: 'Panagia Kara' & 'Europa' over the weekend, 'Women dancing in a field of poppies' today.

Mid-morning on a warm, sunny late October day we drove to Clark Reservation, which is only a short distance from here. This is a small State Park, but spectacular, with a lake – Glacier Lake – eroded by melt water, held between high limestone cliffs. Apparently, the lake's Indian name is Kai-yah-koo ('tobacco satisfies'), deriving from the legend of a mother who lost her child in the lake and would come each autumn to cast tobacco into the water to encourage the Great Spirit to watch over the child.

Dark green water, surrounded by trees growing on the limestone cliffs. Rooks cawing high up over woods & waters in blue sky. The leaves now are a brighter yellow & gold, and there are more on the woodland floor than on the trees. We walked over deeply fissured, water-smoothed, pitted slabs of limestone, & over leaves that concealed the broken rocks. Late herb Robert, small pink faces among grey boulders. A chipmunk, tail twitching, came to sit quite close to where we sat on a rocky ledge, watching leaves drifting down in the sunlit woods.

28 October

> *Primal cultures tend to be tribal rather than idiosyncratic in their psychology. For instance, most North American tribes possess what must be called a 'communal soul' in comparison with the Western precept of the soul as personal property . . . Among the Iroquoian people the power that vivifies the tribe is called* orenda; *and it is this force which briefly animates the members of the tribe. People enrich or enervate the power that gives them life, and then they pass out of existence . . . What remains is the tribe; the community; the* orenda.
>
> . . .
>
> *It is through relationships that Native Americans comprehend themselves. . . . Underlying the identity of the tribe and the experience of personality in the individual is the sacred sense of place that provides the whole group with its centeredness. The Indian individual is spiritually interdependent upon the language, folk history, ritualism, and geographical sacredness of his or her whole people . . . The relatedness of the individual and the tribe extends outward beyond the family, band, or clan to include all*

things of the world. Thus nothing exists in isolation. Individualism does not presuppose autonomy, alienation, or isolation.
Jamake Highwater, *The Tribal Mind: Vision and Reality in Indian America*

If we were less isolated, if we knew ourselves as part of a web of relationships that includes the whole natural world, would we be less afraid of extinction? I think we would, for surely no one wants to outlive *their* world. But fear isn't of personal extinction alone but also of parting from those we love. Is it possible to know a unique being and not wish him or her to exist eternally? Is it possible *not* to assume that personality is eternal? But if we really did belong with one another, if we were centred in a sacred place, we would feel differently about life & death. In *our* world the ego suffers horribly because of its privacy, and what it fears, with diabolic intensity, is its own self-centred, phantasmagoric hell. Does it all turn on whether we are capable of living in the eternal now, in that 'place' where I, for example, live with my mother & my brother & my dead friend – with them, or in the relationships by which 'I' am? 'They're part of us, we're part of them.' Yes; but I can't easily let go of the idea of the soul as the core of being, which we can never share fully with any one, and which joins us in the depths to the Spirit of the Creator, God. Even with all the crimes of our religion upon us, & in the time of its decay, I still retain its sense that humankind isn't *only* part of nature.

Women are empowered by the resurgence of the Goddess. But her rebirth in the late 20th century mind is also in response to fear of extinction, which our excessive sense of individuality exacerbates. She is Goddess of the cycle of nature, of life & death, & of the 'rebirth' which emphasizes creative continuity, but not the survival or resurrection of the individual. Her return, in the lives of some men as well as women, is the great creative event of my lifetime. Yet the corresponding toppling of God, like the statue of a dictator, is good only in so far as it breaks the bonds that bind us to patriarchy. For what remains, as one extreme threatens to replace another, is the task of relating male & female creativity. A task whose difficulty I don't underestimate, in view of the power of patriarchy & the hold of its manacles upon our minds. When the statue has been broken up it will be necessary to know the father again, & not without fear as well as love.

29 October

A Welsh exploration, with David & Kim, on another sunny fall day. First they took us to the chapel in which they were married, a small white-painted wooden building with a steeple, standing alone on Welsh Church Road near the village of Nelson in wooded, hilly country. It dates from 1876 (a chapel built on the site in 1850 burned down) but there are tombstones in the adjacent cemetery going back to the 1840s and probably earlier. Almost all the names on the stones are Welsh: Owen Evans, Mildred Richards, Francis, Parry, Davis, Davidson, Hughes, William Williams Formerly of Llanfihangel Rhos Garn, Carmarthen, Ellianor gwrag T. Jones Bala, Samuel L. Jones lanybyddher . . . How young many of them died!

All so quiet, no one else about, no cars on the road, grey trees bare of leaves in hillside woods nearby, green wild strawberry leaves half hidden by fallen leaves, crunching underfoot, near the oldest tombstones in a corner of the cemetery.

From there we drove on through the beautiful landscape of rolling, glacial hills, by ploughed fields & fields of cornstalks, most of them harvested, & fields where the stalks have been ploughed in and stick up out of the soil, past farms & barns & silos, & one open barn full of yellow corn cobs. We visited Hamilton College (its fine chapel, 1827, designed by Philip Hooker of Albany), where later we would return to an evening of dance & music. Now though we went on to Utica, where David was born. Outside Utica, at Remson, David's friends who are renovating Welsh chapels in the area (there are about thirty) took us to look at a few of them.

Capel Enlli, a small chapel, white-painted wood on a stone base, more like a schoolhouse than a chapel from the outside. Inside, two iron stoves, one on either side of the lines of pews (men sat on one side, women on the other, into the twentieth century). Brown wallpaper, damp, peeling off. I opened one of the two large bibles on the table (the other, *Y Bibl*, was shut with clasps) and read Leviticus 20:13 –

> *If a man also lie with mankind, as he lieth with a woman, both of them have committed an abomination: they shall surely be put to death; their blood shall be upon them.*

A multitude of dead flies lay on the floor & on the windowsills. The restorers had placed a new image on the outside of the chapel: a Celtic cross superimposed on an outline of Enlli, the sacred island. Surely, the original Calvinist Methodists would have regarded that as idolatrous; they would have had nothing of that.

We were then taken to two chapel sites, where only the cemeteries remain: Capel Bont (Baptist), leaning stones among trees on a mound, & Pen y Caerau, where the first Calvinist Methodist church was erected in 1824. Visiting Capel Enlli & being driven to these sites was a haunting experience. The landscape reminded me of Ceredigion, even of the area round Brynbeidog & under Mynydd Bach: poor ground, small, irregular fields divided by stone walls & rows of trees, many of the fields returning to the wild, others in which the boulders have never been gathered up. A stony stream which the Welsh would call a nant. Not hard to imagine the first Welsh settlers at the end of the eighteenth century, driven from Wales by poverty & restrictions upon their religious liberty, coming up slowly, with their children & possessions, in wagons drawn by oxen, through the densely grown woods.

David's father, who came to Utica as a Presbyterian minister in 1948, had a church downtown but also preached in the outlying chapels. Initially he gave one service in Welsh & one in English, until about 1954 when the Welsh service was discontinued.

The last chapel we visited – it was dusk now, with jets high in the blue sky catching the sun – was the most substantial. Capel Cerrig (Stone Chapel) at Remson. Here there was a gallery from which we looked down on the oak pews, long, curved seats that held the shapes of the backs of the people who had once sat on them. A library upstairs, with many cofiants remembering the lives of nineteenth-century ministers, & bibles & hymnals, & a Welsh translation of *Uncle Tom's Cabin* (*Caban F' Eny-thr Twm*, Remsen, N.Y. 1854).

Inscribed on the outside in stone:
Adeiladwyd y Ty Hwn gan y Trefnyddion (Whitefield)
    Calfinaidd Cymreig
    i addoli'r Arglwydd yn y flwyddyn
    1831
(This house was built by the Welsh Calvinistic (Whitefield) Methodists to worship the Lord in the year 1831.)

As we drove back to Utica the sunset was astonishing: at first pink & smoky purple, then purple, yellow & vermilion red behind the city. In Utica, we met Richard, David's brother, & his wife in a Japanese restaurant, & after an excellent meal, went back to Hamilton College, where Richard's music was among the work we heard in the theatre. Afterwards, to an 'English' pub, The Red Lion, where we stayed drinking & talking until after midnight.

It's the concept of empowering that disturbs me in feminist thinking, together with the narcissism that sometimes results from women's (or men's) self-assertion. But this isn't because I am afraid of women's power, or fail to recognize women have had their power taken from them in male-dominated society. The problem with power is, partly, mine, as a man who shrinks from power & its exercise. I've long been drawn to John Cowper Powys's concept of 'unmaking' – as for instance, in *Porius*, in Myrddin Wyllt's decreation of himself as god & man in order to become again a child of Our Mother the Earth (though even she, he says, can't be trusted with power). It's thus, I believe, we can open ourselves to the forces that make us, and become mediums of a creativity that transcends the world of competing egos.

But the problem is also with different kinds of power: mechanical & authoritarian, in the tradition of torturing nature's secrets from her & applying them to technologies that threaten to destroy mankind; and creative, in the sense of making, birthing, imagining, healing. As these powers clash so we are drawn to take sides in a war in defense of nature & creativity & the planet itself. But how fight without becoming what we fight against?

It's necessary for women to assert themselves, & necessary for activists to defend the planet. Is it disingenuous, even dishonest, for me to say that in not fighting, in refusing to exercise power, I'm contributing to the defense, rather than showing my back to the enemy? Cowardice is what I most fear in myself. But to what extent is the idea of cowardice a gender construct?

No, this is sophistry. I know what courage is, & I know when it fails me. The problem remains that creative power may become tainted or confused with the very power that would suppress or destroy it.

The Welsh who struggled up through the woods to build their chapels and worship the Lord on American soil were strong men &

women, with such life in them though they would have believed their sexuality an abomination. Or would they? Eve the temptress, the door through which sin came into the world. Yet surely they would have been, many of them, kind to one another, & loving, erotic. But didn't their strength as a people, their capacity to survive, depend upon their worship of the Lord, & all it implied of woman's primal sinfulness? And we know it was the women who were strong, as well as the men; stronger, & not only because of their nurturing kindness, but also because of the fierce god, the disciplinarian. They're people I respect, though I know that much of what I value and believe in they would have seen as an abomination. And where shall we find an equivalent strength, to struggle, to preserve & pass on values? In our bodies that we bless rather than curse, in knowledge of the nature they're part of? In our kindness? In the return of the Goddess, now that their God who overthrew her has in turn been overthrown? Or in knowing within ourselves the woman-man, man-woman, which to a society depending on gender differences would have been perverse, evil, destructive of its very foundations?

There's another reason why I think of these things now. Hard to speak of without sounding superstitious; but I am superstitious! So will speak of it. Since living in this house, M. & I have dreamed more vividly than ever before. Why? Because it's on a 'line', or in the country of a people who dreamed, and for whom dreams were real? Surely such a force doesn't vanish, but in some sense, 'visits' those who are receptive, as they may also feel a spirit in the woods & lakes. Or it may be that our very knowledge of those people, slight though it is, activates a human need & a faculty that we, to a lesser degree, share with them. And there is also in this house, as M. says, confirming what I had felt, the presence of Terrie's late husband who is very much alive for her. Even now I am sitting in his study, writing at his desk. There's nothing superstitious about this. It's rather my knowledge that is expanding. As I come to know more about the female & the male in me – the forces but also the mysteries we call by those names – so I also know more about how the dead live on in the living, & life & death mock our concepts of them. We can have access to a different & greater knowledge, which our beings open on, so much more than we dream of in our philosophies.

If female creativity has a biological base (which doesn't limit it or make it exclusively 'material') so does male creativity. It seems to me we know very little about these things – things which are fundamental to our human being – and have scarcely begun to think of them. Or perhaps it would be truer to say that every religion has its picture of them while we, who live among their broken images and have no coherent picture of our own, have still to arrive at an understanding of who & what we are.

Late afternoon & evening: 'Steadily the day burns', 'Palikare'.

31 October
Morning walk by & in the cemetery woods. Cloudy, mild. A black squirrel flowed away over the ground & up a tree. A few late purple flowers on roadsides & in the woods.

Two years ago today we scattered Mother's ashes on the sea at Barton. The last time I took her to Barton cliffs, when we sat in the car because she was too weak to walk, she said 'Goodbye sea'.

I felt that she, like her father, wouldn't have wanted a stone. 'If people cared to remember, they would.'
Later: 'And every cleft is mute'.

> *Sometimes I think I am half mad with love for this place . . . My center does not come from my mind – it feels in me like a plot of warm moist well-tilled earth with the sun shining hot on it.*
>   Georgia O'Keefe talking about her home in New Mexico.
>   Quoted in Elinor W. Gadon, *The Once and Future Goddess*

See Julia Kristeva on women's 'privileged cosmic connection because of their bodily rhythmic cycles' (Elinor W. Gadon).

> *Wholeness is not the hero's journey of individuation and separation, which has been glorified since Homer. In the way of the Goddess the path leads to a consciousness that is responsible to all that is alive. What we have called matter is not separated from spirit; matter is impregnated with spirit.*
>   (Elinor W. Gadon)

2 November

Storm in the night battering trees round the house.

I started writing in the morning and worked until 3, finishing 'She hides her golden hair' & 'A hymn to Demeter'.

Elinor Gadon claims that, 'For 2,500 years, since the time of Aristotle, men have been talking about separation and isolation as the human condition'. I think this is true – though not all men have been talking thus – but isn't it also true that, without separation, there can be no love – or no love other than mother love – and no person to love & be loved? But consider, also, Nicolas Berdyaev's detachment from nature & the female; indeed, the personalist's fear & loathing of any form of merging. We have to understand this male fear, and not only in terms of 'the repression of the female [that] has been a festering wound that has poisoned the spirit'. Could we transcend or subvert dualism without losing our souls? Or without killing desire, by closing what Powys calls 'the great paradisiac division of male and female'? We may come close to oneness, but wouldn't it be a kind of death to achieve it? Indeed, a death that Eastern religion regards as our highest aim? Creativity as I understand it, though, is inseparable from desire.

4-6 November

Friday. From Syracuse on the early morning train, with M. & David & Kim, to New York.

At first through an area of trees standing in swamp water. Glimpse of the Oriskany memorial on the far side of the wooded Mohawk Valley. Utica. Amsterdam. Schenectady. The sky had lightened to blue by the time we crossed the Hudson at Albany, where the train stopped for half an hour and we got out onto the platform.

For some reason, in Albany I saw and felt Ramley Road, Morgans Farm & Turville's Nurseries, and experienced again sensations of boyhood, in the womb of place. I thought that it was probably on this very line that Powys, travelling to lecture engagements, wrote portions of *Wolf Solent*, re-envisioning the West Country places of his boyhood!

Hudson widening below Albany. Across mud, water & gulls, white on pale blue, the Catskill Mountains appeared beyond the farther shore. Mud & rock shores, rows of rotten posts descending into the water. Red & green buoys, rock islands with trees, & islands with lighthouses. Ducks, swans, swans in flight, necks outstretched, low over the water.

Rhinecliff. Poughkeepsie.

Still some dark reds & rust colours among bare, grey trees & evergreens on rocky river banks, rising in places into great mounds of rock. Gothic 'ruin' on an island; a prison, more formidable, with its squared stone walls & razor wire fences, than the rock it's built on. Suspension bridges, steel networks, across the ever-widening Hudson. Light with a milky quality between the banks, glittering on waves.

Croton-Harmon. Yonkers. A glimpse of graffiti on tunnel walls – late 20th century cave art, shaped by the urban world.

Penn Station. Sun striking down between skyscrapers, mist of light, blinding above. Glimpse of the Empire State Building. Taxi to our hotel, the Barbizon, at the corner of 63rd Street and Lexington Avenue. Tall buildings carrying the eyes up, sky-reflecting glass; gilded skyscrapers. This is New York as I have sometimes visited it in dreams, standing between tall, shapely buildings or looking fearfully from a high window (as from our hotel room, though only on the 16th floor, with towers rising high above it, and a man on a ladder – dreadful occupation! – against the side of one of them, above).

In the afternoon we walked to Central Park. Crowds of people enjoying the unseasonable weather – 15 degrees above average for the time of year. Many with something to sell: paintings, massage, a Vietnam story. Many disconnected, intensely self-absorbed, but many families & couples too. Nothing I had read had prepared me for the islands of rock, the huge formations outcropping in the Park, grey rounded backs, smoothed, & scored, & gouged by ice, breaking the grassy surface. Once, presumably, such rocks must have been removed from the surrounding areas of Manhattan, where high buildings overlook the Park. I climbed onto an outcrop and saw the power of the flowing lines inscribed by the crushing, grinding, ploughing ice.

From Central Park we walked to Fifth Avenue. Passing a group of black break-dancers performing vigorously & athletically to an appreciative crowd outside the Plaza Hotel, we had a brief look in the foyer, taking in the opulence. New York is a feast for the senses, a rich feast that I, a mere spectator, could have gone on enjoying, though in places, with garbage on the streets, it sickens.

Near the Plaza Hotel we came upon a Miró sculpture, a big horned piece of black, polished bronze, outside a soaring building of black glass, with a slightly concave structure that carried the eye up, and gave me a momentary sensation of vertigo, even though my feet were on the ground.

At the Museum of Modern Art I made the mistake of beginning in the wrong place, with (mainly) European paintings. Even so, it was wonderful to walk among them, despite the fact that I saw only a few.

Cézanne: *Self Portrait in a Straw Hat.* How unassuming he looks, how ordinary, I'm tempted to say, a man who makes me smile in fellow feeling, but then see the seeing eye! Cézanne's fruit, his *Pines and Rocks* – the painting that made the strongest impression on me – in which one can sense (not just see) which are trees, and which are rocks, because the painter renders the essential substance of each, creating in paint images – is that the right word! – for the bodies we know in the world – or don't know until we see them with senses wakened by the painter.

Picasso's *Boy Leading a Horse* & *Les Demoiselles d'Avignon.* What a telling juxtaposition! Boy & horse seen with respect & love. Women rendered in images of bestiality & allure – soulless beings – different aspects of woman to the eyes of the male. Where our modern vision begins: a liberation; yet also, for man the image-maker, what can be release into another prison, from perspective & representation, into his interior world of hatred, fear & lust.

Of course I tried to see too much and it was as I was looking at the Brancusi sculptures – the wonderful *Bird in Space, Fish, Magic Bird,* & the golden 'eggs' of *Madame Pogony* & *The Newborn* – that my unease increased and I began to articulate it. Unease at trying to see too much, & therefore not really seeing anything properly. Unease at being in a museum & playing the part of aesthetic consumer, rather than responding to art as an artist, as for instance William Carlos Williams did to Juan Gris, making his own work at the imaginative interface, stimulated & supported by other artists alive to the visionary & formal challenges of their time.

But it was also unease at having begun and, on this occasion, ended with the Europeans, whose work is, in a sense, out of place, instead of looking at the work of Americans, who responded to this civilization, manifested in the city around us. Museums are necessary: they make great art available to anyone who can afford the entrance fee. But they are also, in a way, dangerous places, which abstract works of art from the life of the times & from the process of creation. Far better, if we can, visit an artist's studio, or a gallery where the artist lived and worked, dedicated to his or her work. The main reason why I was so disappointed by our visit to Bolton Landing was because the place seemed completely untouched by David Smith. Here he had worked, yet no sign of his work remained.

Later, as we walked back to the hotel after a good meal in an Italian restaurant, the sky was clear and we could see, beyond the lights of airplanes, one or two stars shining in the spaces between skyscrapers.

Saturday. By subway to Strand Book Store – more folly of book buying, including a pristine review-copy of my collaboration with Lee, *Their Silence a Language* – then by taxi to Battery Park. Here, on a building opposite the U.S. Custom House, were the coats of arms of many cities, including Southampton. The buildings in the immediate vicinity are grand, mainly brick buildings of the late 19th & early 20th centuries, some of which were probably offices of the great shipping lines. Behind, the World Trade Center & tall buildings of black glass, in which we see the older brick buildings mirrored, their images rippling as we walk past.

By Battery Park to the waterfront, trash in green water lapping against stone breakwaters, a few men fishing, the Mariners' Memorial, an expressive sculpture of three sailors from a torpedoed ship, abandoned on a life raft to the sea. Then, looking out across the waters of the harbour, I saw her, the Statue of Liberty, image imprinted on my mind from countless films, & which, in the first instant, I felt I was seeing with other eyes, eyes of multitudes of immigrants, as they sailed in for the first time. All in the same moment, the famous words stirred to life in my mind:

Give me your tired, your poor,
Your huddled masses yearning to breathe free.

Later I would look up the quotation, which I felt rather as an emotional shape than remembered word for word, and was astonished by the third line: 'The wretched refuse of your teeming shore'. But at the time the words woke in my mind at sight of the haunting image, raised at some distance across the harbour, but giving an impression of gigantic size &, to me, deeply moving.

We walked along the waterfront, looking at Ellis Island & the Statue of Liberty and came to where crowds were waiting for ferries to take them to one or other of the islands and a group of black athletes were entertaining them, turning somersaults & standing on their heads. Then through Battery Park – alive with pigeons & grey squirrels – & after a beer in a bar, round to the United States Custom House (site of Fort Amsterdam, built in 1626), which has recently been converted to use as the National Museum of the American Indian. The administrators of the Museum are well aware of the ironies, and exercise great care in presenting the exhibits as things belonging to the life of the people who made them, rather than merely aesthetic objects.

Again I saw a few things: images of animal spirits, dolls, masks, pots, hats, garments, a ghost dance dress (most poignant), a boulder with incised design following its contours. And found a few words:

> *Every object has breath.*
> *A fisherman knows the direction of the wind by listening to the singing of the birds.*
> *"My father explained this to me: 'all things in the world', he said, 'have souls, or spirits. The sky has a spirit; the clouds have spirits; the sun and moon have spirits; so have animals, trees, grass, water, stones, everything. These spirits are our gods; and we pray to them and give them offerings that they may help us in our need.'"*
> Edward Goodbird (Hidatsa), *Goodbird the Indian, His Story*, 1913.

The works of art – to their makers necessary parts of their lives, participants rather than objects – were alive, breathing. In a different way, I was equally fascinated by the building: a monument to commerce, as a Museum leaflet describes it, & a massive piece of imperial architecture, each exterior column decorated with a head of Mercury and its entrance pedestals bearing sculptures representing America, Asia, Europe, Africa. Inside, opulent marble; 'nautical motifs – shells, marine creatures, sea signs'; and, most expressive to me, round the rotunda dome, a series of murals depicting the great ocean liners & working dockyard scenes.

Initially, I assumed the artist had assimilated the new world of business & heroic energy to the spirit of the early explorers, also depicted between the modern scenes, and had thus worked in the spirit of the architecture, which in scale, design & quality of materials likens New York of the ocean liners to the classical empires. But afterwards Kim told me the murals were the work of Reginald Marsh, who painted them in

1937, as a project commissioned by the Works Projects Administration (WPA), initiated by F. D. Roosevelt. This threw a different light on the murals, without negating my original perception of them, since now their majesty appeared in ironical contrast to the time & circumstances in which they were painted.

From the Customs House we took a taxi to Chinatown and asked the driver to take us by a route with a view of Brooklyn Bridge. He did, on a road that virtually took us under the Manhattan end of the bridge. Looking at its powerful & graceful curves & steel spiderwork, I thought of the Mohawks who had worked on it, and who bestrode many of the highest towers of New York, walking on girders suspended high above the ground, as fearlessly as their peoples had once hunted and gone to war. The new moon, fine as a steel shaving, curved in the sky above the bridge.

I thought, too, of what Barbara, who once lived in New York, had told me about her recent visit, when she had seen the city against a vivid sunset, and felt its magnificence, its awe-inspiring grandeur as a human achievement, and at the same time had seen in or behind it an image of Babylon & other great imperial ruins. As she described the image to me, I felt she had seen something similar to my perception of Berlin, with the bombed & gutted city inside the new structures, though she had seen the future while I, perhaps, had seen the past. But although I could sense what she had seen, and recognize its possibility, I had no intimations of apocalypse.

Time was running out before our train back to Syracuse, and after a meal in a Chinese restaurant, we took a taxi back to the hotel, and from the hotel to Penn Station, and the Arab taxi driver sped and wove skilfully through the traffic, getting us to the station with half an hour to spare.

Occasionally, from the train window, I glimpsed strings of lights stretched across the Hudson, illuminating suspension bridges, but, for the most part, dozed or slept until the train, which was bound for Chicago, got into Syracuse at 1 in the morning.

What I feel now, after the visit, is that we have almost set foot in America. It made me aware of how rural upstate New York is, even Syracuse, a populous city, but in which one is more aware of trees than buildings. Easy to understand how, to a New Yorker, the city could be the world.

That's true of many citizens of big or great cities, of course. Amsterdam, or Paris, for example. New York though is so completely urban; even in Central Park with its primal rocks, one is under the eye of buildings on either side. And it is both a great modern city and the idea of modern urban civilization: the image that, to my knowledge, no other modern city quite equals. Once or twice my mind went back to Berlin, where I felt how impossible it was to escape history, how we were caught up in & shaped by our times, even when we felt relatively immune. In my glimpse of New York – a glimpse of small parts of it – I saw rather the individuality of people. Not the uniquely personal: that's hard to see except with the eye of love. Rather, manifestations of the idea of individualism: each one a self-maker, some a failure in worldly terms, who get to sleep on benches, but are as obdurately singular, or more so, than the successful. I have found a good deal of openness in America, but also a firm determination to be oneself & to 'make it'; a sense of respect due; & a widespread difficulty among white people of imagining being otherwise. I begin to see why socialism has never been alive as a popular idea here. Neighbourhoods do – or did – produce a sense of community, which dies with their decay, or diminishes or becomes unrealizable in the minds of those who rise above their early economic conditions and move away to another part of the city or another part of the continent.

And, maybe, in the absence of communal belonging, the city itself becomes the amniotic fluid in which one lives, supplying all one's needs, or one feels with others, equally disconnected, a kind of fellowship. I can imagine loving it; either growing up to love it, with the knowledge of a taxi driver for the streets, & the knowledge of a bum for the pavements & corners; or loving it as a stranger who comes to it, and, in a world whose poverty or oppression has cast one out, finding the means to live, & the freedom to make oneself. Even in bad times, or perhaps especially then, the latter should never be forgotten, for it's more than a dream, despite the many whose dreams have come to nothing.

12 November
It's distinctly chillier now, but not cold. The exceptional fall weather continues, with sunny days & open skies. Sometimes overnight a light frost.

Black & grey squirrels are active among the trees about the house.

One morning I saw a bright red object moving through the air – an apple, in the mouth of a grey squirrel.

Later: 'Verdun' (reshaped). 'She descends into the dark'. 'Christ is risen!'

I feel now the 'Demeter' sequence is finished. It was quite unexpected. I hoped to write one or two poems about Crete, that's all.

In the evening we drove to the airport and picked up Elin & her friend Jacomien, who are here for a two-week visit.

13 November
In the Everson Museum of Art, in downtown Syracuse, Andrew Wyeth's *Hoffman's Slough*, 1947. The shadow of the hills has spread almost completely across the valley of the Brandyvine. Beyond the far hill his father, the painter N. C. Wyeth, was buried in the Quaker graveyard. The shadow spread 'like the eyelid of night,' he said. 'It all had death moving in.'

I had always had this great emotion toward the landscape and so with his death . . . the landscape took on a meaning – the quality of him.

How could it be otherwise? But how easy it is to forget: the world is that 'between', where we find each other, & where, even if we want to, we cannot lose the dead.

In the evening I started to read Mary Casey's journal, *A Net in Water*, and was at once drawn into it, and into her life & mind. It seems to me beautifully written, with the pleasure of truth to perception, which shapes each phrase & each sentence.

It was with my adult mind that I wrote 'the womb of place'. But it was the boy in me who saw and felt it.

14 November
Walking round Green Lake we get into conversation with an old soldier walking his old, grizzled dog, which is called Riley. The old man is wearing dark glasses and smoking the stub of a big cigar. He tells us he was a lieutenant in the army, and was parachuted into Holland. He took part in the Battle of the Bulge and was wounded. He says some of the German soldiers they captured were only ten years old. He grew up near Green Park and has known the area all his life. The time to come,

he says, is very early in the morning, when eagles & deer & foxes may be seen. All the creatures we see are a woodpecker, then a chipmunk, then another one, tail up, quick, stopping to lift a dead leaf into its mouth. Afterwards we see two more chipmunks, & a golden-green fly on a purple thistle. Wind on the water darkens it, but it is aquamarine at the edges. It is warm in the woods, clouds are high against blue sky, and sunlight gleams on bare trees, silvery grey, with evergreens – white cedars – close to the water.

From Green Lakes Park, M. drives us to Chittenango Falls. This time we walk down the steep path near the Falls and see how powerful they are. The water roars, flowing over a series of 'steps' that it has made at the top, dashes over a precipice and plunges down and over more 'steps' at the bottom. Spray smokes from the falling water and the foam is white as snow. When it reaches the bottom the river, compared to its headlong plunge, seems slow, and crawls away, green & white, over rocks. Then, again powerful, it flows away down the valley, washing over rocks or winding between them. A fisherman passes us, climbing back up carrying his rod & tackle & a string of four freshly caught trout, the shine of their life in the river still bright on their skin.

Returning through Cazenovia we pass the white-painted Presbyterian church, which is as immaculate as the foam. When we stop by the lake I learn from a plaque containing historical information that the Oneida Indians called the lake O – wah – ge – ha – ga, 'where the yellow perch swim'. All the land here was theirs once, though they had a different sense of 'belonging'. Then the Holland Land Company took over the land (it says 'purchased', but that's another problem word) and Cazenovia, named after the land agent, was founded in 1793. We saw four ducks on the lake & a gull, crying. An old wooden dinghy with holes in it, filled with stones & dead leaves & with reeds growing up through the bottom, lay in the water against the shore.

Looking back towards Cazenovia and seeing the white church steeple, and with the Indians in my mind, who had other uses for places and called them other names, I thought of a painting I had seen in the Everson Museum of Art: one of Edward Hick's versions of The Peaceable Kingdom. In the foreground children & wild animals with kindly eyes. In the background, on the shore of a lake, a group of red skins & white settlers, in 18th century clothes. One of the latter, a man in black who looks like a minister, stands with his arms spread out, at the centre of the group. He appears to be uniting the red men & the white, and he may be bringing the word of God to the natives. In any event he is an impressive figure. I thought of him now as I looked at the white steeple, and as we saw other steeples on the drive back to Syracuse, and felt just a little of the terrible strangeness that had come upon the people who were here before, and something of the extreme complexity of loss & gain, when one religion & culture displaces, or partially converts, another.

18 November

On Wednesday, we went to Niagara, with M. & Elin sharing the driving. On the way, we took the road that passes near the Finger Lakes (which we glimpsed at Skaneateles, Geneva & Canandaigua) and crosses the Genesee River. The light was restful, pearl grey & a lovely pale blue to the north.

From Buffalo we crossed Peace Bridge into Canada and drove beside the Niagara River, a broad, powerful waterway which was bright blue – brighter than any blue we could think of to describe it – under a clear sky, and with geese & ducks & gulls near the shore. Approaching Niagara, and all of us, for some reason, expecting an anticlimax, we saw what we took to be smoke rising from the river ahead. But when we came to the Falls they took our breath away. We parked nearby, as if under the rainbow that seems to have one arch in the spray, and vault the road, and walked across to the Falls, spray wetting us like a shower of rain. The perfect rainbow was mirrored in the water immediately above the Falls. But how give an impression of the power & beauty & shapeliness of the Horseshoe Falls, & the roar of the falling water, all at once – here distinct, there hidden in a white cloud of spray. The colours changed as we watched, blue & green among the white water pouring over. Nothing could extinguish the beauty or diminish the force, not even the tourist shops with their trash of Niagara gifts & images in the building alongside the Falls. It was from there, in a restaurant on Table Rock, that, looking across to the American side, we saw the moon, a day from full, through mist of drifting spray.

Yesterday, on another bright late afternoon, with the full moon in the sky, I set out to walk home, after my day's teaching, but got lost among roads between the college and Genesee Street, and walked for an hour before finding the way back to my starting place. Today the breeze is as warm as spring. Elsewhere in the States the weather has been violent – flooding in Texas, hurricanes on the eastern seaboard – but here, day after day, it has been unseasonably calm & sunny, making it difficult for us to believe in the winter to come.

19 November
My main reservation about Ted Hughes's *Shakespeare and the Goddess of Complete Being* so far (after reading the Introduction & Chapter 1) focuses on his treatment of the myths underlying Catholicism & Protestantism, and neglect of Christianity as a new thing. I'm prepared to accept his findings as a mythologist, & his perception of Shakespeare as a writer with a mythic imagination. What I wonder about is Shakespeare's Christianity – not his attitude to the Goddess & the sacrificial god, but his belief in the Redemption & his sense of sin & suffering. Hughes reads myth as a modern, and he reads it with a religious consciousness that is itself mythic, rather than Christian. To what extent Shakespeare was religious, in that specific sense, is a question impossible to answer with certainty, and it is, in any case, rarely asked nowadays. I feel bound to ask it, however, less in response to a pervasive 'spirit' in the plays, that may be felt to be Christian, but more as a result of theological questions, in *Hamlet* & *King Lear* for example. These questions, it seems to me, are the really difficult ones for us, since our modern preoccupations obscure them, while drawing us to common sources of religion in myth.

One of the influences that keeps me at a certain quizzical distance from Hughes's argument is David Jones, who was at once deeply read in myth, and a man who saw 'the New Light' and believed in the unique historical revelation, and a devotional poet. Ted Hughes, by contrast, is a poet in the tradition of Yeats, who exploits (and to a degree constructs) myth for its imaginative potential; which is not to say he, or Hughes, lacks a sense of the sacred, but that it differs essentially from the Christian vision. And doesn't the way of myth ultimately limit the sense of possibility, as, in however many different forms, the same stories repeat themselves? Doesn't it exclude the unique the absolutely other, as in spirit the Christian revelation does not, though in practice it's been used to justify hell on earth & in the mind.

What I also note in Hughes is a language of power, which, in his empathy with energy in animals & in the universal circuit, makes him the poet he is: a male poet of the nuclear age. Not that he's without sensitivity – far from it – but I have a certain sympathy with R. S. Thomas's view that there's not much spiritual sustenance in his poetry. There are other qualities, great qualities, but he is not a Blake in mythic imagination, nor a poet of the most sensitive discriminations, and it's in these, as well as in the power circuit, that life is to be found.

In this book though he writes with an imaginative & intellectual range that perhaps only Robert Graves among modern English poets could equal. Indeed, *The White Goddess* is, palpably, an influence on Hughes's Shakespeare book & its interpretation of English history, though to my mind, at present, the latter is the more deep-delving book.

> [S]omething has happened in the last ten or twenty years [written in 1979] to alter human consciousness . . .
>
> . . . the feminine ground which the masculine overshadowed is now becoming evident. For many centuries the male aspect was dominant in Western thinking to the point that the female was virtually unnoticed. Literally and figuratively she was background; she was the darkness. Now, however, the focus has shifted so that attention has begun to fall on the shadow and the boundary between what was thought to be light, clear, positive, and masculine and what was thought to be dark, mysterious, negative, and feminine.
>
> Joan Chamberlain Engelsman, *The Feminine Dimension of the Divine*

20 November
Early start for our drive to Cape Cod on a bright morning. Little traffic on the roads. On the limestone ridge & descending to Albany, a wonderful view of the Adirondacks. Then, from a diner outside Albany, a view of the Catskills (like a Malvern profile). On to the Massachusetts Turnpike, in similar hilly wooded country, rising to the Berkshires, whitish grey leafless trees & dark green conifers, naked rock showing through. It was not quite dark when we arrived at the cottage we've rented for a few days, in woods of stunted oak & pitch pine, near Harwich.

21 November
In Provincetown, out of the tourist season, many shops boarded up, between the summer crowds and winter storms. A choppy sea in the harbour, gulls hanging on the wind. After sitting over a good seafood meal in a harbourfront restaurant, visiting shops & walking in the streets of the town, we walked on Herring Cove Beach. Darkness falling, waves coming aslant the beach, arrow marks of gulls' feet in the wet sand. Dark sea empty except for one fishing boat making for Provincetown, then another set of lights, & another, & another, the boats coming in at nightfall. The sea breaking on the beach showed the power, now contained, with which it shapes the Cape.

22 November
On Nauset Beach on a brilliant, cloudless morning, sun shining on the sea. As far out as we could see the ocean was blue-black. Big waves rolling in broke with manes of white spray, & in the spray, fleetingly, rainbows appeared & disappeared. Seagulls – wing curve, gliding, ocean riding – you can see how they are made for it. Near where we walked the sand dropped several feet to where the waves, exploding in foam some 20 yards out, came racing & swirling in, eroding the low cliff. Looking back along the beach I saw light shining on the waves, that seemed to close over it, breaking in tumbling white foam & streaming hair of spray, then reforming – but never the same – to catch the brilliant sunlight. But there's no describing it, the sea's body, the Protean sea, its constant formation & dissolution – which is which? – in the surf. Nevertheless, as I looked & listened, images & lines of sea poetry rose in my mind – T. S. Eliot, Robert Lowell's 'A Quaker Graveyard in Nantucket'. We found crab-shells, red ones, bearing the white, ghost face, and I noticed, for the first time, pointillist design, red dots on a white ground. Sand in shell & in eyeholes, dead things, but utterly a part of the element to which the living creature belongs. A wrecked lobster pot, a collapsed contraption of wood & string. Boat shells, clamshells, fragments of white & purple quahog, from which the Red Indians made wampum. Strangest of all, a half lobster, inside eaten out, & mussels clustered on the underside. But what is strange that comes out of the sea? If anything is strange, we are – the Pilgrims who sailed along this shore in another November, or I myself, taking notes in a hopeless attempt to capture one drop of

the movements of light & water, the seabirds riding the swell, or diving . . . Why should we think death brings knowledge? If it does it will be knowledge of death. The knowledge of life is for the living, and is little enough. Between the overarching blue sky & the dark blue sea, we felt we were walking on the blue sphere, on Earth itself, as we were, and as we rarely feel. One small puff of cloud appeared in the sky, and dissolved even as we looked at it. Later I saw another, dissolving, but momentarily very like a whale.

This was what I had come for, to walk by the Atlantic Ocean. But the experience was not as I could have anticipated.

Afterwards we drove to Osterville and found ourselves in what must be one of the most expensive areas of the Cape, with large houses close to the water. But there's an air of prosperity about all we have seen, of comfortable good living built over shifting sands. In the Rest Room of the restaurant where we had a meal I stumbled on a well-dressed man standing with his face leant against a corner of the walls, and afterwards heard him say, desperately, to the woman with whom he was sitting at a table, 'How could you do this to me now'.

23 November
Bright morning but a colder edge to the wind. First we visited one of the sweetwater ponds near the cottage – ponds formed in kettle-holes are a feature of the Cape – where waves were rolling in. Gold light where it touched the sand underwater, between leaves washed to the edge & darker water, under the wind. Geese rocking on waves.

Then we drove to Plymouth Plantation: a place of 'living history', where the replicas of two villages have been created, the 1627 Pilgrim Village & Hobbamock's Homesite. The first was a neat piece of historical imagining, more evocative for the wind blowing dust & smoke & straws through the dirt streets, & between the wooden houses. I was less taken by the idea of actors playing the parts of 17th century pilgrims. The Indian site was more impressive, partly because, as one of them was quick to point out, the guides were not actors, but descendants of the Native People. It's on the site of a village whose inhabitants were wiped out by plague, before the Pilgrims arrived, and where they found the Indian storage-pits of food, which enabled them to survive the first winter.

We emerged from one of the bark-roofed houses to a light flurry of snow, which we first thought was ash from a fire. The make-believe of the Plantation was well done, but, for me, elaborate recreations inhibit imagination, making me think of our need to make replicas & costume dramas of the past, and it's incidentals (if they can be thus described) that are evocative – a cock & chickens scratching in the dirt around the wooden houses, the view of Cape Cod Bay over the fence, the sight of a Bible on a table & the thought that these were indeed people borne up by the word. It's the fact of their world being gone that comes alive for me – the world of the early settlers, as distinct from the physical & spiritual foundations they laid in New England. It's the emptiness I feel, but also, countering it, an image of my boyhood fantasy (a fisherman's dream) of a simpler communal life, close to the sea. Today it was the weather that conspired with imagination, as we went on to Plymouth harbour & Mayflower II & Plymouth Rock. As we walked on the decks of the wooden ship, creaking at its moorings, flakes of snow blew round us, still light, but on a colder wind. And the sky, which had been almost cloudless in the morning, was swirling & smoking with blue & grey cloud over Cape Cod & the coast. If we no longer share the faith of the dead, it's perhaps a sense of the elemental conditions they knew that enables us to feel with them.

24 November
Thanksgiving Day. Cloudless, cold. We saw on TV that 3 inches of snow had fallen at Syracuse yesterday. Heavy traffic on the Massachusetts Turnpike until the New York exit. Tusks of ice suspended from rock beside the road. A sprinkling of snow on the countryside from about 60 miles from Albany, & enough remaining to suggest a real snowfall as we travelled north. White against blue sky & dark blue hills: an indescribable brilliance. (Again & again I want to find words for beauty & its many manifestations, for the feelings it causes & its many 'external' effects, and for the wonder & mystery & sense of revelation (but of what?) that are part of it. And always words fail me (and I fail words). We stopped at the same restaurant outside Albany, overlooking the city & in view of the Catskills, where we had stopped on the way down, and I had my Thanksgiving dinner of turkey & pumpkin pie, which, as I might have expected, was a disappointment! Interstate 90 West follows the Mohawk

River from Albany to Utica, and there was snow on the banks. Towards sunset, on an almost empty road.

> *A stranger may easily detect what is strange to the oldest inhabitant, for the strange is his province.*
> Henry David Thoreau, *Cape Cod*

From Coleridge's idealism to Pater's relativism: 'the Victorians lost the transcendental sense of nature that allowed the Romantics to perceive significance in the most minute grain of sand. They therefore gradually came to perceive nature as a collection of disparate particular forms with nothing to offer but the experience of their own sensations.' (Carol T. Christ, *The Finer Optic*)

Carol Christ describes an experience in the poetry of Browning and Hopkins that she calls 'the good moment'. In this 'man does find revelation of a transcendent reality through the particular. The experience resembles and in fact anticipates the epiphany of Joyce or Woolf, in which an intuitive flash suddenly invests some common object with visionary experience'. In Joyce's 'epiphany' and Woolf's 'moment', however, the experience is secularized, and quite consistent with atheism.

Another angle on the subject would relate the affirmative paganism embodied in Keats's idea of Beauty to the neurasthenic disintegration of Health (wholeness) and Beauty that Edward Thomas seems to have experienced. And between him and Keats would stand Richard Jefferies with his dual sense of the eternal moment and of beauty in nature too quick for the mind to hold, and which hurts the human eye and heart . . .

I'm aware of some of this history when reflecting on the problem of describing beauty, and if I'm dimly conscious of it, it's in my blood, where it's compounded by modern difficulties with abstractions, and is thus, for me as for other modern poets, one of the fundamental poetic problems. A problem with language, that is, and therefore a problem that pervades meaning.

Yet what I do have is a sense of wonder. It is revelatory, and it contains awareness of connectedness – both the 'thing' as it exists within & by the web of life, and my experience of it, shared with those I'm close to, but also common to my kind. Thus there's much more to a perception of beauty than a response to surface attractions or even an idea of the thing in itself. The minute particular is not an isolated atom, for there are no isolated atoms; it is rather a node – is that the right word? – a centre, within the natural web, & within the human world. The danger of perceiving it solely as the former is the danger of naturalism, while sole perception in terms of the latter tends to cliché. What I seek to articulate in this sense of the thing is creativity: nature as creation, & the creative principle in the human mind. More I can't say, and I'm aware of a great unresolved question in what I have said. Every thing is uniquely itself and more than itself: that is what the beautiful instance reveals. The sky over the mountains – to take a sublime instance, which may easily become romantic cliché – that is at once the result & expression of interacting universal forces, and an impression that will never be exactly repeated, and a thing uniting us, which illuminates the mind and pierces the heart. It is both above & beyond us, in every sense, and part of the fabric of our common world.

28 November
There was snow again on Saturday, but only a light fall, when Elin & Jacomien set off for a turbulent flight across the Atlantic. But this morning was mild, even warm. As I walked back from college, finding my way this time, it began to rain, and rained heavily as I walked through the cemetery. There I passed men with a mechanical digger making a grave. Not quite like *Hamlet*!

2 December
Clark reservation. Tall thin leafless trees reaching up into sunlight & blue air. Now the squirrels' dreys are exposed and a large wasp nest hanging like a paper lantern from the branches of a tree, out of reach. Sounds of trees creaking, groaning. Tap tap of a woodpecker on dead wood. Nothing moving in the woods except grey squirrels, an occasional wind-driven leaf (was it a chipmunk?). Surprisingly, one bright yellow butterfly.

The major defect of Ted Hughes's argument in *Shakespeare and the Goddess of Complete Being* is that he depicts Shakespeare's 'myth' – which turns out to be mankind's primary myth, as activated by English history in the 16th and 17th centuries – as a closed system, in which the key relationship is *within* man, between his soul and nature, rather than between individual men and women. In other words, for all his reverence for the Goddess, Hughes leaves little room for the woman as an *other* person. This fact, together with his consistent language of algebraic Equation, and his humourless forcing together of elements of his pattern, considerably weakened the impact of the book for me.

Yet it does contain many brilliant insights and, more than that, it is not infrequently profound in its treatment of fundamental issues, religious and historical and psychological, as well as mythic. Hughes finds the underlying history of Shakespeare's England – the history 'drawn through the solar plexus', and shaping 'the common dream' of every Elizabethan – in the struggle between the new Puritan spirit and the old Catholic spirit for 'the English soul'.

It's not only the English struggle, perhaps, but the struggle of modern man. But whether we can save ourselves from fatal self-division by being absolute for Nature or the Goddess of Complete Being, I doubt. There's something in the claims of nature to resist, because it spells death for the unique person, the other, and for any possibility not contained within the natural cycle. Ideas of resurrection & transfiguration – I've no right to any stronger word than 'ideas' – are more *poetic*, to me, than ideas of merging and becoming one with. I suppose this is one reason, an intellectual reason, why I cling to the idea of a personal God, even to the unpredictable & terrible Yahweh, because He is not Nature, but capable of doing anything, as Nature is not. It seems to me that it's upon *not* knowing the other, precisely because he or she *is* other, that interest depends, and love.

I understand our need to deify Nature, to treat Nature with love and respect, in order to reverse the history of torture that has made us planetary destroyers. But it also seems to me that *our* common dream – the modern emphasis of the dream we inherit – is a dream of losing one another, in the spaces between us, and eternally, which springs from the death of the soul as a *super*natural principle. Somehow we need the creativity symbolized by the divine breath – that most gratuitous of acts – as well as the creativity of Nature.

5 December
A wet, misty morning, which I began sourly, complaining to M, who is feeling very unwell, about friends who haven't replied to my letters or written to me since we have been here.

The day continued grey & wet – such days have been rare enough in recent months to seem abnormal – but I saved myself from wasting it by taking notes, on *The Tempest* & *Coming Up For Air*, for the last classes of term.

In Bowling/Orwell's portrayal of Little Binfield before the First World War I see images of my own childhood, in the later forties & early fifties, well after the time when, according to Bowling, the possibility of such a country childhood had gone for ever. (As a result of our myths of Old England the impossibility of future childhoods, as their authors had known them, is widely implied in modern English writing.) Of course, a great deal had changed. But perhaps what Orwell was too fearful & too embittered to see, in 1938-39, was how resourceful the child is, how active in joy, & how absorbed in his world as a playground, if conditions allow. There is a danger in books about childhood, especially English books, that nostalgia for the past, & failing powers in the present, will deny the principle of life in the child, as authors, having grown old & disillusioned, project their feelings onto the future, and effectively cancel life itself. Few opportunities for being selfish & self-absorbed equal that of a man reminiscing about or recreating his childhood!

7 December
Eerie dawn, a fine wet snow falling continuously, straight down, snow covering exposed ground, thickening on leafless branches & giving jagged white edges to the evergreens, which are darker for the contrast, a cavernous dark green within the spectral light.

9 December
I clear snow from the verandah and scatter seed for the birds. Chickadees come & red finches & slate-coloured juncos, a small dark bird with a white belly, common here but new to us. Also grey squirrels, furry tails curved over their backs.

In the afternoon when I walk in the cemetery a fine, cold rain is falling. The men with the yellow digger are at work again, scooping up earth and depositing it in the back of a pick-up truck. The place has an austere beauty – white snow & grey roadways between the plots & bare trees that are almost black against the snow & the grey sky. Somehow the drumlins covered with snow seem to rise more abruptly & bulk larger than they usually do. Every tombstone has a smooth cap of snow. The snow near the woods is marked with deer slots & one set of human footprints, disappearing among the trees.

> *If we think that we know about sex and death, together with the reasons why poets connect them, because Freud has told us, we shall go hopelessly astray. We know little of either yet, even as physical facts, let alone as mental ones. What we have to realize is that there are sound reasons for connecting them which are not psychiatric but biological. It has been said by scientists that the two of them entered the world together. So long as an organism reproduces itself by simple fission, death is an irrelevance. As soon as there is differentiation of sex and reproduction on those terms, with the corresponding individualization of the organism, death follows. [Cf. Von Bertalanffy,* Problems of Life, *& Michael Polanyi,* Personal Knowledge*] It is this deep biological connection which Rilke inquires into, as Keats also did.*
> Elizabeth Sewell, The Orphic Voice

'Poetry is a form of power.' So Elizabeth Sewell begins her wise book. I can accept her definition of Orpheus as 'the figure of poetry as power', because it is an exploratory, interpretative power and the nature to which it corresponds is fertility and growth and the cycle of life and death. She emphasizes the *shaping* power of poetry and nature but does not dwell on mastery, which is the idea of power to which I react with fear & revulsion.

It seems a shame to me that Rilke is Elizabeth Sewell's example of a twentieth-century Orphic poet, the more so in that she recognizes his limitations – his inadequate awareness of suffering, his 'passion for abstraction [which] tends to vaporize his poetry'. It is awareness of suffering that justifies the distrust of poetry among some poets whom she criticizes. In Keats, for example, or in Auden or Tadeusz Rozewicz, poets whose moral sense reflected their witness to suffering, irrespective of whether they themselves were victims. How can we now, after the death-camps & in knowledge of daily atrocities, trust a poet whose witness is less?

But this doesn't mean the end of the Orphic tradition – Orpheus experienced ultimate loss, dismemberment; he is also a figure of suffering – or the end of praise poetry. The mistake is to think that praise excludes awareness of suffering and evil. It doesn't in the Psalms, or in the best of the Welsh poetic tradition, in which praise is an expression of love & honour, in the face of utter loss. (David Jones reinterprets both epic & praise poetry in *In Parenthesis* and *The Anathemata*.) Nor does praise necessarily exclude the other tasks Elizabeth Sewell assigns to poetry. How would one not tend & foster language, how not learn & teach, when attending to the qualities of a person or thing? To praise is to be involved with questions of ultimate value, in the context of life & death. Like all good poetry, it is a way of thinking.

But this is to take issue with isolated points. *The Orphic Voice*, first published in 1960, is pioneering work. Has any critic added one word to it since?

> *The human organism thinks as a whole, and our division of it into mind and body is the result of overemphasis on logic and the intellect in near isolation which has led us into so one-sided a view of the activity of thought, so gross an underestimation of the body's forms of thought and knowledge.*
>
>   *'For Orpheus lute was strung with poets' sinews.'*
>   Shakespeare

>   *[T]he Orphic tradition insists all the way through that the mind, in order to think and to interpret nature, must lend itself to what it is thinking about; that thinking is not manipulation but marriage, and in the end between like forms, the mind and body and 'this great frame of breathing elements,' as Wordsworth . . . describes the universe. This is that correspondence of inner and outer landscapes . . . always working, for this is again action and power, and a vision of all the kindred works of creation working at one another, a dynamic concept of a universe working in the sense in which yeast or new wine or, in country parlance, storm-brewing weather 'works'.*
>   'The Orphic Voice'

12 December

A pair of blue jays & two Old World house sparrows – wonderful name for our common English bird – among birds picking up seeds on the verandah. Also a cardinal, the first I have seen, bright red with a black throat & a cocky crest. I spent all morning & half the afternoon reading students' Shakespeare Journals, and was gratified & sometimes moved to see them opening their minds & feeling the impact of the plays. These students are not English majors, & they have no critical theory. They respond to the characters as if they were actual human beings and find in Shakespeare experiences & ideas that relate to their own lives & to present-day society. They sometimes make naïve or absurd comments (I haven't resisted the temptation to collect a few, such as 'Falstaff was a wicked man, because he ate and drank too much and visited Brussels'). But it's so refreshing to find no mere cleverness, no critical superiority, & so much openness & wonder.

Late afternoon, walking with M. in the cemetery. Colder, with a clear sky & a moon more than half-full – a cranium, but I don't associate it with death – brightening & seeming to grow bigger as the light changed. Crystalline crust of snow, sparkling, prismatic, crunching under our feet. Low sun, white through bare trees. Far to the east a very fine line – the Adirondacks. We talked about the magic of the moon, which we feel – enough to imagine how powerful it must have been to people without our science & technology, who saw the moon waxing & waning, & knew it in its mysterious influences. How strange it is to think of *that* power as people felt it on this continent 150 or even 100 years ago – as some people may still feel it – here, where the industrial & technological power was developed that eventually led to the first moon landing. And then to reflect on these comfortable suburban homes, in many of which people don't know their neighbours & seem afraid of them. There are homes that practically no one outside the family enters, and the world comes in only in the form of electronic images. This also is what has been achieved – this emptiness, this fear.

(for the tree of the field is man's life)
Deuteronomy 20:19

I can at times feel strongly the beauties you describe, in themselves, and for themselves – but more frequently all things appear little –

all the knowledge , that can be acquired, child's play – the universe itself – what but an immense heap of little things? I can contemplate nothing but parts, and parts are all little – ! – My mind feels as if it ached to behold and know something great – something one and indivisible – and it is only in the faith of this that rocks or water-falls, mountains or caverns give me the sense of sublimity or majesty!
    S. T. Coleridge, in his letter to John Thelwell, 14 October 1797

[It] is in particulars that Wisdom consists & Happiness too.
    William Blake

Natural Objects always did & now do weaken, deaden & obliterate Imagination in Me. Wordsworth must know that what he Writes Valuable is Not to be found in Nature.
    William Blake

John Armstrong juxtaposes the quotations in his book, *The Paradise Myth*, where he writes about English Romantic poets' (and especially Coleridge's) espousal of passivity, and the contrary examples of Blake & Keats, who, throughout 1818-19, was 'engaged in working out a more severe alternative ideal to that of identifying himself with the realm of "Flora and Old Pan"'. Armstrong's book centres upon the ancient image of the snake-encircled tree, and his argument, in brief, is that the tree, which stands for continuity & rooted order, and the snake, which symbolizes the venture to the marginal extreme, and dissolution of *any* system, are necessary contraries of the human mind. The greatest poetry & art – *The Tempest,* Giorgione's *La Tempesta, Paradise Lost* – are products of imaginative energy born of interaction between these contraries.

18 December
Patches of first snow left in the woods, on masses of damp leaves. But a mild, grey day, sky briefly breaking to blue. Crows cawing to each other, squirrels seeming light as air, rippling, flying over the ground. Christmas decorations – red bows, wreaths, a glittering blue ribbon – on tombstones, and electric lights in shapes of stars & Santa outside houses. We feel homesick; the vacation, which has barely begun – I'm

still marking papers – feels like a hill to surmount, and, once more, I'm counting the months before we return to England. At the same time, I know I should be making use of the opportunity to write.

The other evening we entertained German guests. Christina, who is a psychologist, & Dietland, a professor of Zoology at Syracuse University, who has been on many expeditions to Antarctica. They left Germany to come to the States thirty years ago, and now live in a house which they built in the country, with 100 acres, mostly woodlands, in which there are many kinds of birds & animals, including coyote. As they said, this is the kind of space one can have in America (given a good income) but not in Europe. We started to talk about education, among other things, and how little students nowadays, in America (but in Britain too), know about European civilization. Dietland told us something about his childhood in the country, near Dresden, and about the Bomber Command raid that destroyed the city. He spoke of his recollections of buildings opened up, and destroyed, leaving only some small sign of the personal life they had contained, and of messages scrawled on walls, informing relatives & friends where the survivors had gone. This led me to recall my memories of Southampton after the Blitz. And, suddenly, I thought, here we are regretting how little our students know about European civilization . . .

I saw the irony; and at the moment that was all I saw. On reflection, though, I can't see that ignorance of the great books & ideas is any less of an impoverishment. But I'm too aware of my own ignorance to want to dwell on what my students don't know. And aware, too, of how much intelligence & sensitivity they bring to the things of their world, including TV culture. My greatest regrets about my own education, in fact, are that it gave me no science, no knowledge of natural processes, in particular, and almost no understanding of music. Nor do I think it was all good for me as a writer to focus, so early & entirely, on the *written* word.

> Lorine Niedecker
> 'took a lifetime
>   to weep
>   a deep
>   trickle'

> Some days I see
> what a fat mouth I am.

Men attach themselves to this world as certain kinds of seaweed cling to the rocks by the seashore. They care little about life eternal, for like the ancient from Ithaca they do not hunger for the truth or for their heavenly homeland, but only for the smoke of their earthly homes.
    Clement of Alexandria,
    Quoted by Hugo Rahner, *Greek Myths and Christian Mystery*

19 December
Morning. Snow falls fast, small flakes; then slowly, larger flakes, some like pieces of tissue paper, drifting. Again the ground is white, the verandah & the round table, now propped up against the side of the verandah, & branches, roofs. Then the sun comes out and there are tiny snowflakes – glittering points – that seem to be dancing up & down & sideways, instead of falling.

21 December
Another day of bright sunlight. Walking back from the college along Radcliffe Road my long shadow went striding before me. White sun, which the high ground & pine trees in the cemetery hid from me for a time. The news from Frome is that our neighbour has had a breakdown, and is in a psychiatric hospital. Walking opens my mind & heart & I think of him & his wife & little children, who adore their father. And I remember Charles[3] who died on this day – St Thomas's – in 1980, in the afternoon, as Sue & I were driving with the children from Wales to be with him.

> *'The belief that the written word is charged with thaumaturgic power is of very ancient origin; in fact it may be traced all the way back to the graffiti of the Neolithic civilization and even to the cave-art of Paleolithic times. This phenomenon stems from the untold power of the image: imo – ago, "to rouse from the depths".'*
>   Boris de Rachewiltz, in *New Approaches to Ezra Pound*

---

[3] Dr Charles Hope Gill, my first wife's father. My poem in his memory is included in *Master of the Leaping Figures* (1987).

22 December
Last night was horrible. We went to a Christmas party in the college & sat at a table with several people we had met before & no one wanted to talk but two or three (& one in particular) *performed,* making a loud joke of everything & in consequence any communication except at that level was impossible. Why do people behave like this? It isn't only academics who do it, but I have met it before in academic circles & this is the form in which I know it best, with people who must be at least intellectually able within their specialism, starting away from anything resembling an idea &, what's far worse, effectively refusing to recognize the existence of any other human being or take account of his or her feelings. No eye contact, nothing but manic laughter, idiotic antics instead of speech. Is this how people relate to each other in hell? And why, why do they do it? Sometimes I think the reason is fear. Social clumsiness (which in my case usually takes the form of silence); fear of other people, either fear of ideas (or intellectual competition, which is as ugly as this idiocy), or fear of appearing pretentious or of 'talking shop'. But of course the ugly noise isn't only or mainly an avoidance of ideas, but a refusal to let other people be, in a space in which all can laugh & talk together.

It was something like this that I met when I first went to Aberystwyth. I hated the atmosphere, I couldn't breathe it & eventually it helped to make me ill. Fear is what does it, I know; I don't blame others for being afraid. We're so uncertain of what lies between us. Will the ground give way under our feet? Will we be exposed to ridicule? Or will we reveal feelings that are dark to us, feelings arising from the very uncertainty, from fear that there may be nothing between us, only emptiness?

I was awake in the night thinking about this, & feeling ill – probably because I'd had too much wine to drink – after reading the last few pages of Mary Casey's *Journal*. This too was finally a disturbing experience, because of her pain, & also because of the intensity of her aloneness. This was, perhaps, self-chosen, even an intellectual conviction (her espousal of Plotinus and the flight of the Alone to the Alone). But I also sense in her writing a narrowing, an increasing turning inwards, so that even the wonderful quickness of her perception of nature – birds, weathers, flowers & trees, sun & moon & planets – gives way to an internalization of the outer world, or the world in which she is a creature & part-creator. If this is so, it could be because of the pain, physical & mental – Gerard[4] told me that Mary, like van Gogh, could *not* have lived longer. This isn't a matter for me to speculate about, let alone judge; rather it provokes my interest in the relation between the poetic mind & the world, & in the connection or exchange of energies. I would put it something like this: earlier in the Journal, when Mary is physically & mentally more vigorous, what she expresses is the world in its quickness, as it is alive to her; as she grows older and her health fails, the world becomes somehow *drawn*, & drawn in, by her pain.

When are we, any of us, most alive? When we are quick to respond to the universe surrounding us, which consists of human relationships & ideas & works of art, as well as nature & the elements? Or when we are most conscious of ourselves in our aloneness? All that another can really know – & only by sharing it – is the former.

Christmas Eve
Letter from Lee[5]:

> *It can be liberating moving away from our own place; encouraging universal perspectives and thoughts of wider interconnections within this common moment in western culture. This time of looking back over a thousand years and looking forward to the next.*
>
> *You are right in this sense of time "between". I feel I am trying to understand something about the past five hundred years rather than the last ten.*

'If we dare talk of big ideas,' he says. Why not? This was the voice I needed to hear – to wake me up to a sense of shared purpose, of creative possibility.

---

[4] Gerard Casey, poet, farmer, religious thinker. His poems are collected, together with an essay, 'The Shield of Achilles', in *Echoes* (Rigby & Lewis, 1990). His letters from Africa to his wife, Mary (poet and author of *A Net in Water*), are included in *Night Horizons* (Phudd Bottom Press, 1997). Mary Casey was the daughter of Lucy Penny, youngest daughter of the famous Powys family, which included the writers, John Cowper, Llewelyn, and T. F. Powys.

[5] Lee Grandjean, sculptor and painter, with whom I have worked on several collaborations, including *Their Silence a Language* (1993).

Christmas Day
The fine, dry weather continues from the fall & apart from the Christmas shopping & coloured lights & phone calls to & from family & friends, this hasn't felt like Christmas. So we felt, driving out of Syracuse in the morning – no parents to visit, no children coming to stay – 'a bit empty,' M said, 'like the road'. But in the event it was far from being an empty day that we spent with David's mother, & David & his brother, Richard, at Mrs Lloyd's home in New Hartford near Utica. There were many stories about Wales – Mair Lloyd is from a Welsh-speaking area near Swansea and studied at Aberystwyth – & about the Welsh community at Utica. Stories about people Mair had known – the Welsh poets, Gwenallt & Waldo Williams – & about members of the Lloyd family. Again, the old intimacy – my old friend Rheinallt Llwyd is a cousin of David's – that I sometimes felt almost part of, and never resented because I wasn't; the intimacy that's one of the things I love about Wales. Now it was present again in the stories, but also immediately in the family, & in the house, in the family photographs – David & his brothers & sister, Margaret, at different ages, the children & their father & mother, grandchildren. A family, a house, in which love is palpable. What I felt simply was gratitude. But something else too, as Mair's stories & her speech (her Welsh accent after many years in America) took me back: not desire to return, or regret at having left, but the wish to do something for Wales. A wish connected to writers who are my friends – Emyr Humphreys, Roland Mathias – & to all that I learned to value in the culture & the land. There is, too, the autobiographical impulse, which I keep putting off; the impulse to tell my story, but in relation to the world that living in Wales opened up to me.

29 December
Reading closely in Mary Casey's *A Net in Water* & poetry I have become aware of another 'story', in her love for Valentine Acland, than that of the metaphysical poet whose master was Plotinus. But there is of course no radical disconnection between the two things. Love, as Mary Casey experienced it, was a meeting &, maybe, a momentary mingling of souls, which intensified aloneness in the core of being. This isn't to say it was a bodiless experience – her love poems, as I now apprehend them, are vividly sensuous – but it was, I think, an experience in which desire

was transmuted into spiritual intensity. If I am right about this – and I'm aware that my words are at best a crude sketch of Mary Casey's passionate conscious complexity – then her poetry sprang from her love, and was urged into form by her simultaneous reading of Emily Dickinson. This interests me deeply, because of what it reveals about a creative source.

I feel more for the poetry, with its integral metaphysical quest, in the light of my new knowledge of its complex humanity. There are rare minds that seek truth before all else, and do not allow love in any form to cloud their vision, though they feel it as a power capable of tearing them apart. Emily Dickinson was one; Mary Casey, I think, was another.

Bright, cold day. We drove to Pratt's Falls, between Syracuse & Pompey, where the first mills were built in Onondaga County, in 1796, by Manoah Pratt & Abraham Smith. (Always when we've seen the name on a road sign I've thought of Les Arnold's line parodying Dylan Thomas: 'after the first pratfall there is no other'.) When we got out of the car I found it beard-stiffening, ear- & finger-tingling cold. A clear stream, edged with ice & sun sparkling today, flows out from among tall bulrushes & falls broken white down a sheer rockface into a deep gorge. The bulrushes drew me – they always do; there were bulrushes in the gravel-pit pond at Warsash, which is one of my earliest outdoor memories, bulrushes stood in their magnificence on both banks of the Test at Totton, & as a child I heard the story of Moses in his basket among the bulrushes. Now they drew me to look closely, and as I did so there was a sudden bright flash of red, a vivid flame, as a cardinal came & went in an instant among the tall straw-coloured stems.

A long talk with M. over lunch. Is all love at root mother-love, which nurtures, recognizes the other, sends out into the world, and at last, as matter, receives back the dead? Today, as we recover a sense of the sacred earth, the idea of the soul fades, we have less understanding of the need for transcendence & the supernatural. Are we, then only part of nature? And does creative freedom ultimately depend upon our being made in the image of God? From love we went on to talk about modernism (making it new), and deconstruction. Every subject now seems to lead back to fundamentals. That is where we are. The modernists were almost all religious believers (but not in the same religion), and in their art they sought to make new vessels to carry ancient wisdom. For them, the past was rich & dark with meaning; it was itself – to vary the metaphor – a river, or a number of different streams, for which they had to free or make a passage from past to present. But for us time seems to have a kind of transparency, and we look down & down, as through clear water, to see whether it rests on anything. Almost every glance goes all the way down. It is dizzying; as George Oppen felt, words are skyscrapers – and what is under them? I don't say there's nothing underneath, no foundation; these are only metaphors, words sent out to catch a feeling and bring it into view. And what I feel is that everything, beginning with the human image & descending through every level of identity, is in question. Towards the end of the twentieth century we know less about ourselves than any people have ever known. People of other epochs may (or may not) have been wrong about themselves, but the stories they told themselves, the myths they lived by, were grounded. Our choice of stories (including different versions of religious fundamentalism) seems almost limitless – not one is inevitable. And that's freedom, it's said; you can be anyone you like. But in reality all the masks are mass-produced, and their wearers may find out they are no one. Many people though are concerned with real things – the unreal world, for intellectuals the world of superficial ideas, betrays them into unreality. Speaking for myself, I do not feel unreal, insubstantial (though alone, without M., I might, and I have done in the past), yet I could give a less 'rooted', a less solid, account of myself now than at any time in the last twenty-five years; less solid, I mean, in terms of religion, politics, philosophy, where I belong. So it seems I may, after all, be learning something.

30 December
Last night, in the outside house lights, we watched a fawn-coloured young doe feeding on plant roots under pine-trees close to the house. She took no notice of the lights but went on feeding peacefully, with an occasional quick flick of her white tail. Apparently, she had a companion close by, which we did not see.

31 December
'Bare ruin'd choirs, where late the sweet birds sang.' Peter Milward, in *Shakespeare's Religious Background*, says, speculatively: 'This sonnet, if addressed to the young Earl of Southampton, may well have particular

reference to the ruins of Beaulieu Abbey, which formed a major part of the Southampton estate'. The sonnet has long been one of my favourite poems, and although no local connection can affect its quality, Milward's suggestion, which associates it with my original home ground, delights me.

Did Shakespeare wander with his noble patron in the New Forest and hunt (not poach) the deer, and note the yellow autumn leaves, and charcoal-burners' fires, close to the abbey ruins? That was where I saw my first Shakespeare play, *Much Ado About Nothing*, among the cloisters. It was a summer evening, and I was sitting on a chair in the open, with fellow pupils from Rope Hill. I was wearing short trousers, I remember (and feeling it was high time my parents bought me long trousers, such as my companions were wearing). The play enchanted me, but all I really remember is being conscious of my bare knees.

About that time – long before the Beaulieu Motor Museum was thought of, and thousands of people began to visit the site – I went there with my father on one of his official calls – probably, when he was advising on the establishment of a Beaulieu vineyard – and, wandering alone, in the quiet, I found a broken white eggshell, a pigeon's, in a crevice of the ancient grey wall. I loved such places from boyhood with a physical passion. The Norman Sheriff's house at Christchurch was another. The look of weathered brick or stone & the moss or small plants growing on it; the textures, which I seemed to be able to feel even without touching them; the smells; the warmth or cold. I had a passion for such things, an appetite, a longing to be near them. Later, I found in my reading others who shared it (later still, I recognised it as a danger: 'the sludge of nostalgia'), but, as far as I am aware, no one taught it to me. If anyone, it would have been my mother – Dad cared little for history – with her love of romantic historical poems, from Palgrave or *Laureata*, which she recited or read to me.

When I look back, though, I seem to have been drawn to ancient textured things – stone axes, mammoth bones, stonewalls, clay pots, gravel pits, earth & clay & chalk – from very early on. But the truth is I don't remember when I first responded to the poetry of words, whether it was before or after the Blitz, from which time I recall my feeling for things.

Which comes first, I wonder? Doesn't John Berger describe seeing as primary? But do we really see, or feel with pleasure the curve of a thing, before we have a word for the object or sensation? Isn't feeling first, or feeling & taste (&, perhaps, hearing) *together*, as we suck at our mother's breast & she murmurs to us? I have a very strong sense that that is where love begins, and that, with love, knowledge unfolds; in which case neither seeing nor words are primary, but taste & feeling are. Words though in the cave of the mouth come with these senses, as well as from hearing. Our bodily relationship to the world is closer, & perhaps quite different, than is commonly dreamed of. And it is more of a lover's relationship; so that, for example, in what at first seems absurd & grotesque – Goethe's (or John Cowper Powys's) idea of making love to the earth – there is, in fact, a profound truth. There's also the consideration that if we are earth, made of clay, we have every reason to love it and cleave to it with passion, unless we're distempered by self-hatred. And that, of course, is part of the story; an important part, but not the whole, which requires knowledge of the breath of spirit.

How satisfying that the first writings known to us should be on clay tablets.

New Year Day 1995
To begin the year, M. & I walked round Green Lake & to Round Lake. Cloud hanging low among the trees. Rain dimpling the water, which was grey except in a few places at the edges, where the beautiful turquoise could be seen. A day of round waterdrops hanging in rows from twigs & from buds & thorns. As we came to the first lake there was a loud cawing, agitated & aggressive, coming from high in the trees, &, looking up, we saw a large brown hawk on a tree top & a crow flying at it, furiously cawing, & driving it into the air. Mallards & a flock of Canada geese on the water, which was so still that their wake showed like vapour trails in the sky. Then we heard a loud rhythmic knocking from among the trees. We had already glimpsed woodpeckers but the noise was so loud I didn't immediately associate it with them. But then we saw one, a big, black-backed bird with a red crest (a pileated woodpecker, I learned later), and watched it working up & down a cedar, hammering its long beak into the bark. There was ice under the damp surface of the path & we had to walk with care. Cloud light as mist among the cedars & drifting across

the water – grey on greeny grey, diaphanous & at the same time utterly real, water of water, earth of earth.

'Written in clay'. 'The Mother of Laussel'.

EARTH SONG CYCLE

Women dancing in a field of poppies

Slowly at first they measure
their steps as the sun strengthens,
the poppies flame redder,
the sea-blue deepens, and they,
women in white, loose-limbed,
flowing, circle hand in hand,
turn faster, and faster,
leap and fly till their feet
are birds, white birds, skimming.
And round they go, wing to wing,
as the field revolves and the sea,
and earth veils and unveils,
white and blue, under their heels,
which skim and pause and come to rest
while round and round them turns
the scarlet field,
     and O the earth.

She descends into the dark

For now she knows nothing
but terror, rage.
     And what she throws off
is the scent of it, the reach
of the stamens that beckoned,
the face of the flower

that drew her in, and closed,
as a sundew swallows a fly.
                    Beyond this,
the meadow spins in her mind.
She feels on her hands the hands
of her friends, gripping,
torn away.
                    It is a lost world
she sees in the dark
and nothing more, not the god
whose sweat she smells
and breath she feels on her face
as he drives her down.

                    Later she will see,
but now there is only his breath
mixed with the reek of horses,
the smell of roots
and engulfing earth.

How can she know what visions
will be born of her story,
or even if it is true?
There is, perhaps, no power
but hers, no god to command.

This is not the moment to see,
nor the moment of those
who will follow, seeking her
under the ground.
                    How many will come
as the light fails, or the glare
extinguishes sight.
                    How many
will plead with her
for annihilation
or beg to return.

          Only now
the dark has taken her
and she has left, to her friends
reeling apart in the meadow,
and her mother, listening
to the echo,
        only a cry.

And every cleft is mute

A cry echoes among the mountains.

             Somewhere
the earth has opened. Where?
Where is her daughter?

She searches and searches
but finds no sign.

Who cares? Not the god
who leaps and dives and plunges
to death in ecstasy
and forms again among the foam.

Not the stones she kicks over,
or the cuttle-bones
or globs of tar.

Not the roots she finds
sodden with salt –
       images
that would bewitch her,
grotesques
with human form.

Are these, maybe, a sign?
She calls again
and no one answers.

The sea changes.
It is clouded glass,
into which she looks, and sees
nothing.

No one. Every cleft
is closed against her call.
She sets her bleeding feet
on shells, weed, foam.

Turning over, the waves
are cavernous,
smooth for an instant
and full of sand.
                    Light rides in
on crest and underlip.

The day will be immaculate,
the night perfect, that sees
her torch wandering in blackness
like a moon.

She hides her golden hair

Let him bellow,
                the thunderer
wrapped in cloud,
for this, she says,
is only the beginning.

        Birds
returning to her without a message

drop dead from the sky,
snail shells bleach in heaps
spiralling down to dust,
snake and green lizard
crawl into holes to die.

And she hides her hair
in a hood.
    As a stormcloud
falls on the harvest,
blackness blots out the gold.

    She walks alone
among her people, searching
their sightless eyes
for a sign.
    No one answers
when she calls and calls.
Men break picks on the fields,
oxen strain to shift the plough,
seeds fall on soil turned to stone.

    She will waste all
as she is wasted,
calling and calling.

Ovens and storage bins,
the giant pithoi
that poured out bounty,
all their round bellies
hold emptiness and mould.

And this, she says,
is only the beginning.

    Afterwards
the fall of ash,

seas white with corpses,
no swellings on earth
but the bloated dead.

      Let him look down
on his handiwork,
            thunderer,
father of desolation.

      Who will survive
to make an offering
or give him thanks,
when she, who brings
all things in their seasons,
provides nothing,
and no one but the dead?

A hymn to Demeter

Pardon us
that we will
our end & forgive

the poet
his ambition
to stand alone

on a high peak
surveying
the waste.

Take the map
from our hands
which we take
for the world

& let us be
where earth
and waters meet

& make, for you,
a song.

'Christ is risen!'

Again the priest
has cried aloud
in a joyful voice
to the people
who move off together
carrying candles,
a procession
of white moons
threading the dark.

Once more a cry
sounds where a cry
has echoed
over corn field
and olive grove
across thousands
of years. Again
the cave stands open
and the faithful see.

Written in clay

What could he do, the swineherd
gaping at the meadow?
      Had he dreamed
the earth had opened, closed,

his herd gone squealing down
along with her,
              the fairest flower?

What could he do but wait,
and learn, maybe, that flowers spring
from rotting flesh.

*

She will come back (they said),
the sweet, red seed is on her tongue,
she will return
and we will taste her words

            And when she rose,
she will descend (they said)
she will descend again,
and rise
      there is no end,
spring air returns,
the birds repeat their calls,
the wind of winter wails
in trees and round the house
the same old song

              no end
                    no end

*

He looked (the squeal
still ringing in his ears)
and every thing
            everywhere
spoke to him of her

She was the water and the fish,
the stream within the stream
becoming flesh,
she was the black grain and the bread,
the wet clay and the pot,
the light, the dark,
the silence and the word,
she was all formless
on the verge of form, and form
becoming formlessness.

And so he tasted on his tongue
the song
and sang it to a lute
made from his flesh and bone

and wrote it in the clay

                        no end

                                    no end

2 January
A little snow overnight, powdering the ground. It was fine in the morning when we went for our walk but later snow fell again, softly, floating down. I put out seed for the birds and a large bird with a red breast (an American robin, a kind of thrush) came to a bush near the house but no closer. I worked all day on 'Pictures of Bruges'.

3 January
Slow snow dance in sunlight, flakes floating down, up, sideways, across each other. Sun white behind thin cloud.

6 January
Snow was falling dryly, tiny pellets, when I walked in the cemetery, climbing a hill where the ground is sown with rocks, to my favourite tree, which stands on the summit and branches vigorously from its trunk.

And from there, looking down the other side, I saw that a funeral was taking place, not far below me, though I could barely hear the sound of the words. I quickly stepped back out of view, and walked on the other side of the hill to the woods. Low cloud overall but a more than usually clear view under it, to the line of the Adirondacks patched with snow.

7 January
Heavy snow overnight, ground covered in the morning, a still, white world with dark objects silhouetted against it; clouds full of snow, and snow falling lightly all day. Fall skies continued until very recently; perhaps now the winter we have been promised will begin.

I have been writing almost continuously since the New Year, expanding 'Pictures of Bruges' and writing the two Rembrandt poems, 'Homer Dictating', 'Remembering Berlin', 'Ode to Antonio Gaudi', 'Two Figures in Catalonia', 'Towards Arras', and 'The Stones of Brittany'. Without my journal to draw on, with images & sensations I would otherwise have forgotten, I doubt whether I could have written any of these; yet each must also be new, now, felt & seen anew, if it is to live. Some don't, of course; but I don't think I've written many duds.

I learned in *Time* about John Osborne's death, which set me remembering the first I heard of *Look Back in Anger* (before I saw or read it), in connection with a librarian, at Lymington Library, who seemed to be the only intellectual in the whole place – that's the meaning of the memory – since he gained notoriety by defending the play, possibly in a letter to the local paper. It's strange to think how much has changed since those days – even in Lymington, though the change is double-edged: who would care enough to argue about a book or a play today?

Thinking about John Osborne also led M. & I to talk about writers & the public expression of strong negative emotions, such as hatred. Whether this takes courage (as a form of honesty), whether it's the main or only source of creative energy for some writers; and whether such obsessions are symptoms of a dying culture. My personal stake in the subject is my extreme tact, which I sometimes feel has had a profoundly inhibiting affect on my writing; though it could also be that I've simply no talent for the 'confessional', and can only write from experience when I loosen the grip of my ego, and bring the experience under a certain light. Instinctively I strongly dislike what I think of as writing that betrays intimate personal experience: but then I also sometimes regard it with a sneaking respect, or (if I am blocked) envy. My ultimate feeling, though, is that, if we're to understand ourselves & the world we live in, we must transcend the intimate details of our life story. But that doesn't mean being impersonal, but learning to distinguish between the personal and the egoistic. I want to be able to say 'I' in a poem with feeling, with the whole of my being behind it; it's one of the things I've found most difficult to do, probably because I've often failed to make the distinction. When thinking & feeling in terms of ego it's impossible to write with one's whole being: which is easier to say than to act on.

Towards Arras

From Picardy and the land of the Somme
the late summer sky had lowered,
become a roof of dark blue cloud.
And it broke in downpour, shattering
on roadside memorials and regiments of graves,
smoking across the fields,
the mounds and ditches, that already,
after seventy years, look prehistoric.
And as we drove towards Arras,
slowly, against the pounding
and blinding cloudburst,
I thought of Edward Thomas
and how he would have loved
the violence of this passing storm.

20 January
The weather became mild again a few days after the snow, and continues mild, almost like spring. Record temperatures for the time of year; weathermen ascribe the weather to a giant pool of warm water in the Pacific, which releases warm vapour into the air, and produces rainstorms in California. I went back to college on Tuesday, and have begun courses on Advanced Poetry Writing & Modern British & American Poetry, which promise to be stimulating, as well as on Shakespeare, which has started with more student participation than I was able to elicit last term. On Wednesday I rewrote 'Pictures of Bruges', partly in response

to workshop criticisms, which confirmed my misgivings. Today, Friday, I have written 'Hieratic Head of Ezra Pound'. The problem is to do any kind of justice to such a subject. Pound gave so much; I am one of many who are indebted to him. But there is also a painful contrary truth: as Peter Ackroyd says, Pound's 'paranoia was the same as that which, in more powerful and determined men, led to the construction of Auschwitz and Dachau' (*Ezra Pound*). My ability to write at all about the subject was fuelled by indignation with Pound scholars who see no problem, and treat his Pisan experience & the poetry it produced as redemptive. In my view, Pound, having helped to make modern poetry possible, proceeded, by his implication in fascism, to call words (and poetic 'vision') into question. But he wasn't alone in that, of course; and poets who abetted Stalinist tyranny were equally irresponsible.

Hieratic Head of Ezra Pound

Scholars will speak of vision,
even, without irony, 'the final vision'.

The mind of Europe
founders among its ruins.

Words must fail.

The man looks up. The light of the stockade
glares in his eyes.
He is guarded, and displayed.

There is no shadow for him here,
unless it is memory
peopled with shades:

      Gaudier
in his studio under the railway arch,
a man of the renaissance,
the air between them alive with ideas.
They dispose of an age of statues,
a trash of books.

The poet is quick to give.
The sculptor works on the marble,
winning every inch
'at the point of the chisel'.

Naturally, the sculpture
will survive the carver,
and outlast the model.
It will gaze back down the century,
over the work of other men of order
whose material is flesh and blood and bone.

The Head looks impassively over the ruins.
The poet looks out
towards the mountain, beyond the Pisan cage.

21 January
'Vincent': possibly the last of my 'European' poems, for the book.
    In the evening we entertained Sean Dougherty, a young poet taking a course at Syracuse University, and his wife Suzanne, who is an artist. It was late by the time they left, and we had talked & drunk a good deal.

> *[It] is only when the older, more intense belief in the gods tends to flag by the fourth century B.C. that romantic, picturesque poetry, nostalgically descriptive of landscape delights, like the idylls of Theocritus, makes its appearance, to be joined later by some tentative landscape painting. Again, it is only when the gods finally begin to die completely out of the land and when many human beings begin to live lives totally divorced from nature – at the beginning, that is, of the modern age – that landscape painting, picturesque architecture, and landscape description, like that of romantic rediscoverers of Greece itself, become the obsessive themes of art.*
>
>   Vincent Scully, *The Earth, The Temple, and the Gods*

Vincent

In the north
he goes among the people,
farmers, women who cut the peat.
He is a peasant-painter labouring
to paint peasants.

He is somewhere in the room
with them, struggling to paint
the hands they dig with,
and put in the dish, and share out their portion.

                Darkness
comes out of the earth in the north.
It moulds the figures,
it shapes the farms.
This is the good soil of Holland,
the soil the poor live on.
It means hardship, not misery,
not the dry, dusty wind of the Borinage.
The cold wall of the church
chills him to the spine,
he is a servant
of the man-forsaken god,
a light-bringer
who loves the dark.

Earth is new in the south – bright yellow,
vermilion, burgundy, violet,
sky blue, bright green.
Earth melts, burns with a flame
that does not destroy but restores.
This is the force life lives by,
the force he seeks to enter.

The sun roars in the harvest field.
He holds the yellow note,
the black cypress is a vortex
and the heavens rain down fire.

Gauguin paints him painting sunflowers,
in which he sees himself 'gone mad'.

He paints irises in the asylum garden,
tongues wagging, the silence
loud with shouts and screams.

He has gone out of hearing,
he is somewhere deep in the fields,

a stranger in a foreign land.

22 January
Hung over, I walked to the edge of the woods in the morning. A light dusting of snow overnight, dead leaves & fallen branches mottled with snow on the woodland floor. A day of letter writing: to John Peck & Dick Davis, and my cousin in Australia, who, I learned from a Christmas letter, lost his job in the South Australia parliament, when the Labour government collapsed.

25 January
Awake in the middle of the night, I went to the window and saw a deer, distinct against the snow, walking down the sloping open space away from the house. When there is snow on the ground, we usually see the slots of one or two deer close to the house. When I first look out of the window in the morning, into the spaces between pine-trees on slopes above the house, I always see, come & gone in an instant, an image of Brueghel's *Hunters in the Snow*. What I now realize though is the extent to which this is something I bring with me, from my European background, since the world view of the Iroquois, who may once have hunted among the wooded drumlins, was quite different from anything familiar to me.

It's the *difference* that interests me, after an initial period of taking the compensatory view (as I now see it), by which we find in Native American cultures earth wisdom lacking in our own. Not that I deny the existence of that wisdom, or our need for it. But I'm becoming more aware, first, of the impossibility of comprehending any other people's world view as they lived it, and, secondly, of the elements in Iroquoian culture (anthropophagy, warfare, male/female roles) that do not speak to our needs. I don't mean there are not affinities, or that one shouldn't approach the other culture with knowledge & imaginative sympathy (in other words, respect). I mean rather that neither guilt (at the white history of dispossession) nor identification (willing ourselves to 'become' Native Americans) can help us to approach real understanding.

In order to know ourselves members of the same human family we have to recognize the differences between our world views. No doubt this emphasis reflects my preoccupation with Europe, which is where I have been living imaginatively in recent weeks – and the more I explore the ground of Western culture the more I realize how deeply my thinking & feeling are rooted in it. But this hasn't blinded me to where we are, and at the same time as I've been working on the 'European' poems I've been aware of a new ground forming. Neither 'ground' is entirely new or entirely old, of course. (Nor are they as distinct as I may have suggested – it was while we were walking in Clark Reservation among the rocks & trees that the idea of Orpheus suddenly came alive for me; subsequently I learned about the many versions of an Orpheus myth among the North American tribes.)

It may be that for each poet there's one imaginative matrix, which everything life brings – new experience, knowledge, the capacity to renew, to reshape, to see again – activates. In a sense, the poet is at work on one poem, or, as I prefer to say, a body of poetry. But the metaphor – it's more than a metaphor: the nature of a matrix is to give birth – must not be allowed to exclude the possibility of real change, in the poet & in the poetry, or of the revelation that transforms. The creative process is necessarily repetitive – not in the sense of repeating the same poem over & over, but in reusing the materials (the matter). Yet at the same time it contains, for as long as it remains creative, the potential for transformation & transfiguration.

28 January

Bright days, sun on snow, ground hard & dry where snow does not cover it. I worked all weekend on 'Variations on a Theme by Waldo Williams: Bryniau Presely': an idea that first came to me when I was living at Brynbeidog, although it has of course grown since then. In consequence I've felt my way back into those places – Carn Mieni, Pentre Ifan, Nevern, St David's (and Mynydd Bach) – and wished myself there.

5 February

Wind from the northwest & heavy 'lake effect' snow yesterday & overnight. I struggled hopelessly with a Strata Florida poem yesterday, and today wrote 'Strata Florida' 1 & 2. Almost always after writing, nagging discontent. I almost never feel I have said quite what I want to say – never in an absolute sense. Now I feel this about the book too, in which these may be the last poems. When I looked out of the window this morning, there were flashes of white as wind drove snow among the pine-trees.

Whitman begins his Song 'Hoping to cease not till death'. It's the only way for a poet.

from Variations on a Theme by Waldo Williams

Strata Florida (1)
   for Wynn Thomas

   They did not believe in the world
   yet they built one, drawing a line
   from the centre to the margins:
   from Citeaux and the vineyards of Burgundy
   to the Welsh uplands.

   Rhys Prince of Wales granted them land:
   champaign, arable, mountain pasture,
   for the cure of his soul
   and the souls of those before him
   and the souls of those still to be born.

They expected the world to end,
and it did, not once but several times –
by fire, by dissolution.

At last almost nothing remained
of the visible structure –
stubs of walls, foundations,
a doorway open on clouds, hills.

On the surface, there is little
to speak of the makers – monks,
abbots who were patrons of poets,
princes who set aside the sword,
lay brothers who cut down woods,
built roads, tended flocks of sheep.

Only bare tombstones,
and slabs carved with a cross,
fragments of knotwork:
relics of the great design.

And near the yew that was full-grown
six hundred years ago
when a fellow poet honoured him,
Dafydd ap Gwilym lies.
Old then, the yew is ancient now,
hollow, but still alive –
no ruin, Dafydd's tree,
but rooted in and out of time,
in court song and creation's prime,
in love that every moment makes the world.

Strata Florida (2)

for M.

Hawthorn and rowan and outcrop rock
above us, and an autumn breeze
fluttering your hair,
your red hair, your grey hair.

What did I mean to say
taking you there, walking
among the tombs and hart's tongue fern,
looking into the love poet's yew,
the forest of branches?

Hawthorn and rowan burning
against rock on the hills around us
and your hair fluttering,
your grey hair, your red hair,
which the wind blew into flame.

7 February
Yesterday was almost a white-out but this morning the sun rose golden and the sky was clear. College was closed, because of a power failure. Attempting to walk in the cemetery we found the snow too deep for us, waded a short way, and turned back to walk up the road which climbs over the drumlin. Fir trees laden with snow, as if sculpted on the branches. Smooth drifts against banks & walls. Occasionally snow would fall from a tree – we had seen a fine track, which looked like an unknown animal's or bird's, inscribed on an otherwise unmarked slope, and now, as a tree released its burden of snow, we saw a fragment break away and roll down such a slope, leaving the same fine track (like tears on a face, M. said). Long icicles suspended from eaves; mirrored in a window, like a chandelier visible through the glass. Birch bark looks white until seen against snow that partially encrusts it, and then it appears a very pale yellow-gold. Drifts, mounds: a new white landscape that partially smoothes over the old.

> *[L]anguage is a* techne. *It is a human construct designed to organize something as inexpressible as terror and as intangible as joy into a system of sounds. Language is a form of domestication. But it is not an air-tight form – a poet can use it to take something from nature or use it to give something back to nature with a prayer.*
>
> *What the mythtellers and the oral poets know is that truth cannot be captured in a solitary idea. It is alive and uncatchable. It tumbles about in the polyphonic stories told by the animals and birds and mountains and rivers and trees – not in some taxonomy of their separate identities but in the play of exchanges among them, which is the only way we really know nature.*
>
> *Those stories are still there in the Earth, to be overheard by anyone who has the patience to listen. This act of listening . . . is the opening of an aperture to what lies beyond our species chauvinism and the version of human history on this planet which that chauvinism has constructed for itself.*
>
> Sean Kane, Wisdom of the Mythtellers

'Yet history is real too,' Kane says; but the overwhelming emphasis of his eloquent book is upon the wisdom of the hunters and gatherers, and he sees in the myths of the agriculturalists, after the Neolithic revolution, an inclination to the univocal: ultimately the one story imposed by humans on nature, as opposed to the polyphony of nature's voices. While I find the book rewarding for its own sake, I also find it interesting as a symptom of the new reverence for Nature, the Earth, which is hostile to 'constructs' such as God, when it notices them. The best writers of this persuasion, Kane among them, recognize their own modernity and acknowledge that, inevitably, it both separates them from and affects their presentation of 'Stone Age' wisdom, insofar as it is recoverable at all. My feeling – somewhat hangdog in view of the consequences of our 'species chauvinism' – is that considerably more is due to the civilization (product of the cultivators) that has produced us. Yet I also feel with Kane, and recognize in my own 'primal things' affinities with his. The cave paintings discovered recently in the Ardèche – an owl & a panther among the other species – belong to a world we will never return to, but which speaks to us. And as if from within: not only from what 'we' *were* (so much is problematic in this connection) . . .

Carl Ortwin Sauer, in *Northern Mists*, speculates that Irish monks, leaving Iceland at the advent of Norse heathens, and attracted by the idea of isles of the blessed in the west, may have reached the coast of North America before the Northmen. He argues that they would have allowed their curraghs to be carried by the Irminger current, crossed from Greenland to Baffin Island, and then followed the coast south to the Strait of Belle Isle, and so turned into the Gulf of St Lawrence.

Sauer marks the difference between the Irish and Norse motives for seafaring. The former went in search of wonders and to praise God. The latter were warriors & predators, then homesteaders. Of the 'Irish linkage' to Indian cultures Sauer writes:

> *Early French missionaries in Canada were worried by what seemed to them perversions or vestiges of Christianity. Was the Devil mocking them when they found the cross associated with the service of Manito [Algonquian spirit or force empowering nature], and also used as a design on the body and in crafts? At the great Indian winter ceremonial of the year, strangely resembling Passion Week, a chosen dog was hanged on a cross-like structure, taken down after a time, and carried by mourning procession to burial. The great collective rite was performed annually, it seems, from the St. Lawrence to the western Great Lakes . . . Were the French missionaries in Canada confronted by distorted remnants of the teachings of earlier Christian missionaries, an Irish colony gradually absorbed into Indian culture, as the last Norse were into Eskimo?*

Apparently, 'the voyage west from Iceland is much less difficult than getting to Iceland'. Sauer quotes Vilhjalmar Stefansson: 'The New World was discovered by whoever discovered Iceland. For to reach Iceland you must cross a wide and stormy ocean far out of sight of land, while thereafter you can see westward from island to island till the mainland of North America rises above your horizon'. According to Sauer, this 'statement is only slightly overdrawn. Continuous sight of land may be had by climbing the proper mountain and having an unusually clear day. Under certain conditions of air inversion distant land may appear in the mirror of mirage'.

One of the pleasures of reading Sauer is his factuality: not pedantic dryness, but respect for the materials, which, in his ordering of them, speak for themselves. He is rarely emotional, and then to some effect. A case in point is his comment on John Cabot's landing on the North American coast. Cabot 'did not know where he was and got there by a Bristol ship managed by Bristol seamen, who had been to such shores before. There is a monument to Cabot in England, but none I believe to its people, who made the voyage possible and knew the way. History does not celebrate the anonymous.'

10 February

We went last night to a poetry reading in college by Michael Harper, the Black American poet, and afterwards, with Harper, David & Kim, & Sean & Suzanne Dougherty, to a restaurant in downtown Syracuse. The curious thing about the evening, for me, was that Harper cut me, in spite of the attempts I made to talk to him. More curiously, he talked emphatically about the necessity of listening to other people, and told a number of stories that redounded to his credit as a caring human being. It was altogether an extraordinary performance.

This was the third reading I have been to by an American poet. The others were by Stephen Dobyns – entertainingly anecdotal but nothing more – and W. D. Snodgrass – arrogantly sexist. In fact I found Harper's presentation – he read from a new anthology of Black American poetry which he has edited, as well as his own poems – much the most sympathetic. In retrospect, less so, as the many stories he told about his dealings with famous writers came to seem like name-dropping.

11 February

A myth: a mouth: 'a word uttered, something told' (David Jones). "[T]he main technique of Cro-Magnon art, according to prehistorian Michel Lorblanchet, . . . involved not brushes but . . . blowing pigment dissolved in saliva on the [cave]wall. Lorblanchet . . . suggests that the technique may have had a spiritual dimension: 'Spitting is a way of projecting yourself onto the wall, becoming one with the horse you are painting. Thus the action melds with the myth'." (Robert Hughes, 'Behold the Stone Age', *Time*)

In the same article about the discoveries in the Paleolithic cave near Avignon, Hughes derives 'cave fears implanted in the human brain' (manifested in the Cretan Labyrinth & the Christian hell) from the difficulties and dangers (bear claw marks can still be seen on the walls) of entering the caves. Possibly; but something stirs in us still, which is exhilaration as well as dread, a dim sense of knowledge we can only guess at, some participation in the rhythms & energies of animal life.

With the lengthening light and the snow beginning to melt, there's occasionally just a feeling in the air of the spring to come. A vague feeling, almost a smell – which could easily be buried by more snow. A small flock of American robins and cedar waxwings with beautiful pale golden-green bellies came to feed on black berries on a bush near the house. It was a thrill to see them as we sat at table eating our lunch.

17 February
A milder air with a feeling of 'lift', of things preparing to let go – trees, birds beginning to find their voices. Venturing outside Syracuse for the first time since Christmas, we drove to Verona Beach on Oneida Lake. And found the lake a large flat expanse of frozen water covered with snow: a snowfield with small figures drawing sledges or driving snowmobiles far out, like a Dutch winter scene. Nothing more alive than the creek running away from Chittenango Falls, which were tusked with ice. Lunch in Cazenovia, in the restaurant where we had a meal with Kim & David not long after our arrival in the States, which now feels like a long time ago.

19 February
Sunday morning walk with M. round Green Lake & to Round Lake – both frozen & with a light covering of snow. A still, quiet morning, the only noises crow caws, a woodpecker hammering, children shouting. We walked carefully on hardened snow, but in many places on the hillsides soil & dead leaves showed through. New growth on trees & shrubs.

In a recent letter to me, Dick Davis, who now lives in America, included among the reasons he likes being here 'the real spiritual equality compared with where you and I come from'. I recognize what he means: it's one of the things that I, too, like about American society. And the comparison is just. I miss England, yet I've only to pick up a copy of *The Independent on Sunday* to be reminded of things I dislike, including snobbery. Thus, in last week's edition, there's a review of Anthony Powell's *Journals* that notes Powell's 'penchant for the aristocracy' and describes him as being "amply possessed of a quality he praises in others: 'a pleasant degree of malice about friends". I had almost forgotten about the stifling narrowness of genteel literary England – the fear of ideas, the complacency, the condescension – and back it comes with a tidal wave of tedium. And with it comes the class-consciousness, mine as well as theirs, which is something that doesn't come between people in America, in anything like the same way. But in England it's part of our social element, in the very air we breathe.

How hard it is in England to think and write as a man or a woman, as distinct from someone defined by one's own or other people's class assumptions. Even to declass oneself, as, arguably, John Cowper Powys and George Orwell did, is to involve oneself in matters of class. Indeed the very idea of the declassed 'gentleman' – someone who is honourable, considerate of others, careful of his word – can scarcely escape associations of social gentility, as Powys found. I'm not tempted to idealize materialistic American society with its narcissism and suspicion and (in the narrow sense) parochialism, but it does offer one the possibility to stand up as oneself, spiritually equal to other men and women, and in a measure free. Indeed it is this very possibility that judges the failures of American society from within.

> [O]ne could denominate self-imposed exile as a constitutive quality of the American character itself. Although there is no winning an argument about whether Americans are more alienated than anyone else, one can state with conviction that people have come to America, for the most part, by consciously exiling themselves from a native land. A country formed through self-imposed exile bears the marks of this formation in many spheres . . . We still retain a myth of exile at the core of the American character: we believe that while other people are at home – supported by social, political, and cultural traditions and grounded in metaphysical certainties – we are in exile. As a result of this myth, we feel there is "something missing" in America, something lost, something central to human culture that we have gone without . . .
>
> [S]elf-exile is one of the standard postures assumed by our poets.
>
> Stephen Fredman, *The Grounding of American Poetry*

22 February
M. ill with a painful racking cough. Snow falling in sunlight in the morning: a dance of fireflies.

24 February
I sometimes feel as though I have lived several lives, each identified with a particular place. In the past (and in places without our standard of living in the present), I would, at my age, have been an old man longer-lived by some years than the average, and would probably have spent my whole life in one place. The difference of experience between the two modes – the mobile and the emplaced – is great. Yet I feel, too, a strong sense of continuity, though this may be due in large part to my close association over most of my lifetime with one place, and to the length of time I have lived in other places. I remembered my brother Tony's image of the phases of our lives being like a chain of islands, island falling away behind island in the sea – I was a boy sharing a bedroom with him at Hayford when he talked to me about it, the same room I shared for some years with Dave and which later, divided into a smaller room and a bathroom, was my room alone. The image impressed me then, and I have never forgotten it. Now, though, I would add that the islands are both all in the same sea, and are connected under the sea, as a chain of mountains. But this is a truth that coexists with the distinctness of each phase, the life feeling which is identified with place.

Edward S. Casey, in *Getting Back Into Place*, argues for the priority of place over space and time: *'To be is to be in place'*, a message which he says originates with the Pythagorean Archytas of Tarentum (428-347 BC) in his lost treatise on place. I have always obscurely felt the bonds of being and place, through the body and through relationships – familiar, cultural, social – or it would be truer to say I have apprehended the bonds, known them poetically, in the complex 'matter' of place. It's the philosophy that contains large tracts that are obscure to me.

Now I see that each person lives not in one but in many 'places'. If it hadn't been for my parents, and then my friends, what would my feeling be for the raw shingle of Hurst-spit, the soils, the chalk? Without them, would I have wanted to explore a depth of life in place and the many processes of making? What is a body alone the center of? It is in our feelings for one another that we escape from isolation and enter into other possibilities of place. I had my first intuition of this not in my own case, perhaps, but in that of David Jones, when I felt the existence of the child in the man, and the origin of his hope in universal redemption – the whole creation – in his love for his parents, in the one world they gave him. This doesn't somehow lessen the reach of the hope or diminish the love. It isn't reductive thinking, like the psychology that reduces adult love to infantile dependence, because the mother was once the whole of our world and because we may have resented the father as a rival.

Another thing I haven't spoken of is gratitude for the given. If it is true in any sense that I have lived several lives – and it is only true compared to the countless people who have lived less than one life (infants stricken at birth, children, men & women cut off in their prime) – in short, it is only true in the sense that I have been given immense opportunities, and must make something of them, hand on, be of use. Comparisons are false – it isn't for one human being to judge the *use* of any other. Only in respect of one's own privilege, of the many real possibilities life affords one, is it necessary to make the comparison, and always with a view to using what one has to enhance life for others, to open the realm of the possible. For we live in a social world in which many live by exploiting others, by reducing them to consumers or other functions, by closing their minds and stifling their sense of possibility, by distorting the human image to serve their own ends. Ultimately every creative word is an act in the war for survival against the powers that would destroy us and the world.

Place is directly involved in this war. Not only rainforests and oceans and tribes or communities abandoned to external economic interests but place as the locus of changes that benefit the common world; place in all its dimensions as the site of creative possibility. And now, taking the idea of the common world seriously, we can no longer think exclusively of human beings but have to consider the whole of nature, all things animate & inanimate within the web of relationships constituting the planet and Earth in relation to the universe. I may have begun my thinking about place fed by attachments that I had to outgrow, but I am becoming increasingly aware of its ramifications and depth as an idea central to all our concerns & vital to our survival. As for outgrowing attachments, it is rather a case of carrying them on, and extending them, not of putting away childish things, nor of regressing to childhood and seeking absolute security in a return to the womb, but of the child living within the man *and allowing him to grow.*

25 February
Emily's birthday: twenty today. Strange to think of her living near Southampton Water, where for so long I wanted more than anything to live. Strange and pleasing, as long as she is happy.

Snow quite deep on the ground & falling steadily, gusts of wind blowing it off trees, from which it falls in lumps or like a white smoke-fall through branches. On the afternoon of David's birthday he and Kim drove us in their trooper to New Hartford, where we joined Mair Lloyd & the family for a birthday meal. Afterwards we went with them to hear Richard perform his music & monologue, 'Distractions', at Hamilton College. David's sister, Margaret, her husband, John Bollard, & their children had come over from Springfield. I hadn't seen Margaret since she was in Aberystwyth in 1969: a beautiful young woman with long red hair. John was also there at that time, an American studying in the Welsh Department. Now, sitting next to him at table, I asked him about his work on medieval Welsh texts. In his view, the original *Pedair Cainc y Mabinogi*, composed about 1080, may well have been written at Strata Florida. Rhydderch, for whom *The White Book* was made, in the thirteenth century, was a nobleman whose residence was at Newcastle Emlyn. Dafydd ap Gwilym was related to him and would, in John's view, have known the *Mabinogion*.

Far from the world of medieval Wales, Richard's solo performance was a humorously & edgily self-conscious monologue – 'The point of view is that of a 1990s character going through an aggressive journey of self-discovery' – with which he integrated seven of his original piano pieces. I don't have the words to talk about music, but Richard's piano works move me with their dramatic & lyrical qualities. The monologue courted embarrassment and was at times close to hysteria, but always under control, and Richard enacted it with wit & panache. It would have been interesting to know what the more staid members of the audience made of it – members of the church choir which Richard conducts, for instance. Talking about it with M. & David & Kim afterwards, we concluded that they probably thought that if Richard does it, it must be OK. Certainly the audience watched & listened enthralled and responded enthusiastically at the end.

The evening showed me a side of Richard that surprised me, though it shouldn't have done. He is a sensitive man & a serious composer and I had thought him shy, even somewhat nervous. So he may be, I suppose – the monologue expresses a disturbed & questing modern mind – yet, claiming that he was not an actor, he stood on the stage for over an hour and gave a superbly confident performance, an apparently nerveless impersonation of an extremely nervous character.

Afterwards my mind went back to the eisteddfodau that I used to attend in Llangwyryfon, when I saw, literally, the platform on which so many Welsh men and women develop their ability to perform confidently in public, as singers or speakers or actors. M. and I have become strongly attached to Mair Lloyd and her family (and to Kim); they have welcomed us among them with such kindness & generosity, and we have come close enough for me to be aware of the continuing influence in the family, even the presence, of David's father, who died in the year that Margaret came to Aberystwyth. I know in my own experience that the dead live in those they have helped to shape and who love them – live in what they were & in what they have given. But it is hard to express this knowledge in a world that assumes isolation as the human condition, and dwells obsessively on youth & physical well-being & self-development, at the expense of both the whole life-experience and the bonds between generations. Not that one necessarily needs to express the knowledge, though if it were part of our society, in our bloodstream, we would be much the better for it. It's because so much works against it in the Western world today, in the powerful and insidious image-world created by the forces that would manipulate and exploit us, that I'm not only moved when I meet people who live the knowledge, but confirmed in what I feel to be a defining human experience. This, of course, is ultimately what Wales meant to me, though Wales also absorbed a good deal of my romanticism, because I fell in love with a Welsh girl and, losing her, identified my feeling for her with her country and even her language, which always eluded me.

26 February
Dawn light: the old moon & the Morning Star shining in a sky of perfect clarity before the sun rises, blindingly bright on snow. And it is at the

moment when I see the raw universe – so I perceive it, though warm in a centrally heated room, and looking through a window – that I feel the shell of egotism grown round me, and know the absolute need to open outwards.

1 March

Ash Wednesday. I woke up one night recently and, as I was reading about 'dwelling' in Edward S. Casey's book, *Getting Back into Place,* felt the excitement, words and processes coming alive in my mind, that usually means I will be able to write a poem. And this morning other things came together too, and I wrote 'Imagining Wales'.

There are moments when I feel certain my work is important. It's a dangerous feeling, of course, but it isn't really a matter of vanity. For what I then know isn't that I'm a poet who deserves a name, let alone one who rivals those I most admire, but that my concerns are central, and I'm asking fundamental questions. The Oedipal idea of poetic rivalry I regard as a symptom of the ego sickness that comes with the collapse of ideas of community, between poet and people, and between poet and poetic tradition. (The latter not obviating but requiring creative newness, image-breaking.) I feel more than ever that the poet who can't bring his or her work into the 'between', into the world of manifold connections, will die of it, spiritually if not in fact. The farther I get into my writing, the more convinced I am that we're only beginning to think seriously about human identity, and what we need to do in order to create a living community among ourselves and in relation to the Creation.

How should I know what spiritual death is if I didn't know the risk? My primary impulse is to reach out. But it is a struggle as I write not to lapse back into my ego, and when I'm not writing I frequently retreat into it. Indeed writing is an attending to, an entering into, living processes; it isn't self-consciousness, but consciousness moving among the 'things', apprehending connections, waking to the other. It's in the everyday reverie my ego inhabits most of the time that I exist insulated from the quick of being in others & in myself, but which I reach only by waking from the mundane dream.

The central dogma of Christianity is the dogma of the Incarnation.

In this dogma, respecting as it does both the divinity of the Word and the humanity of the flesh, is contained the whole principle of the Christian aesthetic. The implications of this are endless. Certainly some of them are these: While the flesh is frail, and while nature itself has suffered the wound of sin, the Incarnation redeems the flesh and the world, laying nature and reason open once more to the supernatural. In other words, the Incarnation creates the sacramental vision of reality. The flesh, the world, things are restored to dignity because they are made valid. Existence becomes a drama which, no matter how painful it still may be, is nevertheless meaningful. No detail in the drama is without its wholly unique reality. No thing is insignificant.

Malcolm Ross, 'The Writer as Christian', in *The New Orpheus*

from Variations on a Theme by Waldo Williams

Imagining Wales
for Emyr Humphreys

A peal of thunder, a fall of mist.
Afterwards the sun glares, staring on emptiness.
It ignites an image of fire
on ashen hearths, paints
evacuated rooms with streaks of red,
stains the ruined stronghold
on the promontory.

The machines are shrouded.
The quarries sink deeper
under the shadows of their walls.
The mineshaft is a dwelling for bats.

The man sits on the mound
and stares at his hands.
He turns them over, reads the lines on his palms.

He sleeps and his dream is a coracle
in which he is tossed on a stormy sea
that has drowned the cantrefs.
He peers out, into the spray
that stings his eyes,
and gradually, out of the waters,
a mountain takes shape.
He bows his head over his hands.

He is walking alone on the shore
but is not alone.
He kicks over wrack, examines the guillemot
that flaps like an oiled rag in the wash,
the beached seal with a hole in its side.
He wanders alone thinking of the broken walls,
the silence leaking in,
the men and women who sit staring
at the backs of their hands.

What can he do that they will remember?
He knows that memory is a place
that can be lost, though it lose nothing;
a place where all things remain
to be imagined anew.

He sits on the mound alone
and looks at the lines on his palms.

He sleeps and his dream is a coracle
in which he listens, listens hard
against the crash of waters
storming round and past – listens
where there are no words,
no symbol, no metaphor
to bear him over the torrent,
nothing but courage, and his mind
that listens, listens hard

against the fall of silence
crashing round and past . . .

A peal of thunder, a fall of mist.
Afterwards the sun appears
travelling on its daily round.
The man sits on the mound
and looks at the lines on his palms.

3 March

Edward Thomas's birthday. Around this time the curlews would return to their nesting grounds in the marshy fields towards Hafod Las and Trefenter. No doubt they still do.

Here and now, a bright day, on which I walked in the cemetery, treading on a hard crust of sparkling snow. At a distance, an uncanny silvery fluttering over a headstone – when I got closer, I saw that it was caused by three balloons, which had been tied there. Back indoors, I heard what I had been waiting for: the love song of the male cardinal. The bird with bright red crest was perched on the topmost bough of a pine tree, full in the sun, loudly repeating his lyrical whistling note. I was only able to see him at all by looking out from an angle at which the sun was hidden by the wall above the verandah door.

Joe rang in the afternoon – he keeps in touch faithfully – to tell us about the visit he and Maddy made recently to Rotterdam. Later I finished reading Stephen Fredman's book, *The Grounding of American Poetry*, which excites me more than any book on modern poetry I have read for a long time. It also, incidentally, takes my mind back to Aberystwyth and Brynbeidog, and the days when Bill Sherman persuaded me to 'hear' Charles Olson and attend to projectivist poetics. Bill was completely intolerant of my interest in – or, perhaps it would be truer to say, my obsession with – native English writers (Hardy, Lawrence, Edward Thomas), but he pointed me towards an opening out of what was confining in that interest, at the same time as I was finding a deeper 'grounding' through David Jones.

5 March

Morning sky thinly veiled with cloud. Soft air with a hint of cold. We walked alongside the Erie Canal: green water, a tremor on the surface making reflected branches wave, distorting the sun's silvery-green image. Ice turning to slush at the edges, here and there a piece of ice floating. But as the canal broadened, so it was covered with slushy ice from bank to bank. We saw and heard two or three cardinals singing from treetops at intervals along the bank: two notes, a slow one repeated and a rapid one. *Tuw Tuw Tuw Tuw TwitTwitTwitTwit*. Snow crunching underfoot on the paths but the country mottled, a litter of leaves & soil apparently lifeless, few bright colours beside the red cardinals & dark red sumac 'plumes'.

The Erie was a practical school for acquiring engineering knowledge. Resourceful contractors, surveyors and local workmen planned the canal through a wilderness. They drove stakes, bored holes, felled trees, pulled stumps, blasted rocks and dug in swamps. They built canal banks, towpaths, waste weirs, culverts, aqueducts, locks and gates.

As well as the birds, there's a new excitement among the squirrels, the black and the grey. Now they 'talk' more vigorously with their tails, held in the shape of question marks, twitching, or upright and quivering, and, it seems, aggressively. They are more active, jumping over the ground or bolting up trees, and sometimes they make amazing leaps from tree to tree.

From and in response to Stephen Fredman's *The Grounding of American Poetry*:
Modernism is frequently defined as anti-traditional. But is it? Isn't it rather anti-conventional: a refusal of the immediate heritage & a search for fathering & mothering principles in other traditions, & often in the 'primitive'? When was tradition last 'given' in Europe? Think of Cézanne reworking Poussin; Gaudier drawing inspiration from the Gothic sculptors, Brancusi from Romanian folk art, Chagall from the dream-world of Russian Jewry ... Was it really so different for American poets?

I would be inclined to emphasize their advantages, following the newness of Whitman and Dickinson, and in relation to New World energies. But it wouldn't exactly be in the context of the 'burden of tradition' that I would think of, say, Pasternak, Montale, or Machado.

The 'otherness of tradition' (Gerald L. Bruns): this is central to what I admire in American poets within 'the Emersonian lineage'. A poetry of 'facts' that 'open up to mystery'. Fredman comments that reading Black Mountain poets' correspondence between 1950 and 1970 'makes it clear that the anxiety, the isolation, and the uncertainty of whether poetry was even possible had not disappeared from the American scene by the mid-twentieth century'. But this is precisely the strength of American poetry in the line Fredman discusses (and even more, I'd say, in George Oppen and Charles Reznikoff than in Olson or Robert Duncan, who can appear arrogantly confident). How could *any* poet be certain that poetry is possible after the death-camps, after the Bomb . . .? Conventional poets who seem certain, within the English tradition, are insufferably complacent. Conventional verse (as distinct from intelligent use of traditional forms) is equivalent to landscape gardening, which appropriates nature to the house owner; its constructions are forms of property, and belong to the self that questions neither itself nor its world.

The Maya, Olson observes, 'do one thing no modern knows the secret of . . . they wear their flesh with that difference which the understanding that it is common leads to . . .' His conviction that moderns lack a sense of 'touch' resembles Lawrence's. Paradoxically, their need for touch turned each of them from their common world, from the places 'between' that the democratic Whitman celebrated. Are we to suppose that only Maya and Gloucester fishermen are real human beings? Sometimes, it seems so. Which is perhaps one reason why Olson, who can write wonderfully of simple 'things', can also completely baffle comprehension.

'The only interesting thing/is if one can be/an image/of man.' (Charles Olson) This is one of the necessary statements of modern poetry. Pass over Olson's neglect of the image of woman. What, though, is the image he seeks to be (not as personal identity but as Maximus, man of greatest human potential) grounded on? Not on the soul, 'that peculiar presumption by which western man has interposed himself between what he is as a creature of nature (with certain instructions to carry out) and those other creations of nature which we may, with no derogation, call objects'. Not on the soul, but on the body: 'this structure evolved by nature, . . . the animal man; the house he is, this house that moves, breathes, acts, this house where his life is'. 'This organism now our citadel never was cathedral, draughty tenement of soul' (never Gerontion's tenanted house). Objectism requires disposal of ego, "of the 'subject' and his soul". A man will be of use only 'if he is contained within his nature as he is participant in the larger force'. Then, 'he will be able to listen, and his hearing through himself will give him secrets objects share'.

When Olson speaks thus, I find him moving. He convinces me that he recognizes the 'intolerable way' by which man has come to the present. He knows the 'reductions': 'so much fat for soap, super phosphate for soil, fillings and shoes for sale'. He means 'to begin again', his 'one answer, one point of resistance only to such fragmentation, one organized ground, a ground he comes to by a way the precise contrary of the cross, of spirit in the old sense, in old mouths'. He resists with his own body, 'his own physiology'.

And Olson is a giant, in more than one sense. He has freed himself of soul; he is a Blake (even more, perhaps, a Nietzsche) in liberating himself from traditional opinions, ideas, and 'spirit in the old sense'. He gets rid of Logos and grounds himself on Tao. And, surely, a great deal of the Western intellectual baggage he throws out is well got rid of. Yet, is it with the body, even with 'this house where his life is', that a man (or a woman) resists tyranny? Is it with physiology alone? Isn't *all* that he or she is spiritual, strengthened by beliefs, ideas? Ruysbroek's soul dwells in a 'space' greater than any Olson could conceive: the space that opens on God.

Are we members of one another by our bodies alone? Or is that belief, and all it has led to in our understanding of brotherhood, sisterhood, and the common world, merely a word in old mouths? Fredman comments that Olson's 'secret' runs against the Crucifixion, 'a sacrifice of life that redeems it only outside itself'. But that, surely, is a superficial understanding of the matter. I can understand wanting to get rid of Christianity in response to all the horrors and evasions and sentimentalities that our ideas of it have bred. But the Cross is hardly outside life. And in the sense that it is 'out there' (as distinct from something we have made up) it is truth that man falls in love with, as Eric Gill said he did.

It certainly isn't my wish to sound holier than thou in contrast to Olson or anyone else. My point is, rather, that I find in Olson's thinking about 'soul' and 'spirit', as in Lawrence's, an arrogant impatience. And the emphasis on the natural body, in both writers, has other weaknesses, including a masculinist emphasis.

Robert Duncan's conception of the self 'as a site of wholeness with open boundaries' (Fredman) is more congenial to me than Olson's idea of man as object. Duncan is Blakean in his concept of 'the whole', 'our meaning . . . in the content of the whole of us as Adam', 'our moment, this vision of universal possibility', yet, so far, Olson's poems excite me more.

I suppose it's actually where Olson is closest to Herodotus (himself searching for the evidence), or to C. O. Sauer (investigating the facts of earth processes & of the makers) that I find him most compelling. He would not have assented to the idea of making a shape 'out of the very things of which one is oneself made', in the sense that David Jones meant it, with piety towards religious and cultural traditions. It is, though, as shapes made out of 'things' (including speech) that Olson's poems appeal to me, whereas it is the relative absence of things, and the presence of an atmosphere heavy with egotism and subjectivity, that repels me in conventional British and American verse. Even in great poets, in Yeats and in Wallace Stevens, I feel a certain airlessness, or an opening of the poem inwards, on self-drama in Yeats and on the fictive principle in Stevens, which makes me turn with relief to poets in the Emersonian tradition. As Fredman says, too: 'In both Emerson and Duncan there is an Orphic strain wedded to the Platonic, which renders the poet's imagination a participant in the work of creation'. He goes on to say that, 'from this perspective, Duncan contends that fiction is true . . .' But at this point I don't want to hear about fiction, but to wonder about imagination's apprehension of the real, and in what sense it can be said to participate in the work of the eighth day.

What I have set down are, mainly, questions. But Fredman's book speaks to my needs, both in its argument about 'grounding' and in its quotations from the writers themselves, especially Emerson, Thoreau, and Olson, and from other critics and thinkers, such as Stanley Cavell and Jacob Needleman. Reading it even revives my sense of intellectual community (ironically enough in light of my own explorations of 'ground') and reinforces my confidence as a 'poet of place' and in my thinking about poetry. What Fredman says about poets' prose even helps me to a better understanding of my need to write in this journal, which at times I still find hard to justify, though it hasn't stopped me writing!

All this indicates to me that Fredman and the poets' American concerns are by no means exclusively American. Nor were they at any time, even though dislocation in Europe during this century has brought the Old World and the New World closer together, in a shared groundlessness. For example, I was fascinated to learn that Keats's 'letters discussing the Egotistical Sublime and Negative Capability formed one of the primary touchstones for Olson's thinking'. With this point in mind, one could go on to write a different book. It would include a fuller exploration of the affinities and differences between Olson and Keats, and Olson and Lawrence; it would discuss Emerson in relation to Wordsworth, and Whitman in relation to English writers he influenced (including Jefferies, Lawrence, and J. C. Powys); it would look at 'dwelling' in W. C. Williams and Hardy and other writers . . . Well, this could turn out to be a futile game, as pointless as inventing titles for books that never get written. I suppose what I'm pointing to is *my* sense of tradition.

7 March

A better night after two nights of sleeping badly, which made me feel tired and edgy in college during the day, though I pulled myself up by effort.

Rain overnight had cleared away all the snow by this morning. M. heard the cardinal and I saw one of the pair of mourning doves that frequent the woods near the house. But then it started to snow again, and now once more the ground is white.

Late afternoon: darker than usual. I've worked most of the day on lectures on *Macbeth*. How poignant the scene (I vi) before Macbeth's castle! The time must be evening, but the scene conveys the impression of being in full sunlight – the only one in the play to do so – and is full of sweet air and the presence of high-flying, home-loving birds, 'the temple-haunting martlet'. We know that, through the thoughts of Macbeth and his Lady, the interior of the castle is already hell. But outside, through the minds of Banquo and Duncan, the place is, for a brief time, what it should be, when men and nature agree, and human beings act with honour: a heavenly abode.

I can't understand how anyone could think that Shakespeare's plays signify nothing. He knew well the *experience* of nothing, or nothing as a condition that people can bring themselves to; and perhaps he knew it the more because he knew what it meant to be a 'shadow, a poor player'. But *nothing*, in Shakespeare, stands in opposition to love. We scribble all over him with our nihilism, and so forget that he knew what nothing is better than most moderns do, because he knew the loss that goes to its making.

9 March
Evening: my first reading in the States, with Barbara, at Barnes & Noble bookstore. It was well attended and well received. Afterwards we had a snack & some beers with Barbara and Jack at the De Wittshire Tavern. A student in my poetry writing class, who has also been taught by Barbara, described her to me as 'neat', which is a term of high praise.

10 March
Bright morning after a clear, cold night. Branches turned to snakes of shining ice. A large flock of birds – American robins, starlings, cedar waxwings – came to eat black berries from bushes near the house, and we watched them for a long time with delight. The big American robin with its red breast is like fire against the snow, the slender, delicately coloured cedar waxwing is a very beautiful bird, and in this company even the starling is an exotic in our eyes!

A lively evening at home in the company of artists & poets: Rita Hammond, the seventy year old artist, with more vitality than many a young person, with whom we shared a similar evening some time ago, at her studio & home in Cazenovia; Elaine, Rita's friend; David & Kim; Barbara; Sean & Suzanne. Rita showed us several slide shows: one about woodlands, another made during a visit to London in the 60s, and the last consisting of images taken from her life. Each was effective, compelling attention; a coherent whole. She's a woman of courage and spirit, who lives her art.

Sean brought copies of his new book, *The Mercy of Sleep*, a sequence of poems drawn from the life of St Catherine of Siena, most of them given in her 'voice'. The poetry both evokes her medieval world, with its poverty and plague and religious faith, and burns with a visionary flame. St Catherine herself seems to have become the latter: a pure, clear intelligence & flame of love & prayer, her body nourished almost by the Eucharist alone. The book is a fine achievement: powerful, true to its subject, of which it speaks to us in a language that communicates between St Catherine's world and our own.

11 March

There are moments when I realize how insulated I often am from other people, in a world of books & ideas, that's like a protective atmosphere outside my skin, and know the actuality of experience, other people's & my own, in which we lose & find ourselves. It happened this morning when Mieke talked to me about her schooldays, her friends, the two boys who appointed themselves her protectors after a man had tried to rape her on her way home, her first lover, who abandoned her, pregnant, at the age of nineteen, her abortion. It was the actuality that came through to me – her life, the lives of those people; those times, the times that were, but also the living moment, that which we in fact live. And of course, as her experience penetrated me, so I realized the actuality of my own, which even egotism (or perhaps especially egotism) can seal off. Life, it seems, is what I sometimes wake into, out of the dream in which I exist. Life is what is happening all the time, in the instant, but in which I/we are rarely fully present. And when we are it is wonderfully strange, or, at moments of loss or terror, horribly strange. To know it, in oneself & in others, is the one thing necessary, without which we won't know how to value anything else, or how to be towards ourselves and others. In this sense, I understand what is meant by loving one's neighbour as oneself. And now we are beginning to realize what we owe, also, to our nonhuman neighbours.

12 March

A bright, warm Sunday, snow melting.

The soul as depth. This is what many of us have lost, either carelessly, in accepting the values of a secular world that has no use for it, or through loss of religious faith, or through some intellectual conviction that denies its existence. What is happening now, however, is a reaction against the resulting shallowness & disconnection. It certainly isn't a reaction that started yesterday; indeed I would argue that it's an element within modernism; but it seems to me to be quickening, among thinking people, as a result of the ecological crisis & the nihilism of contemporary intellectual & artistic fashions. I'm aware of it as an observer, but first, as a participant; and, in as far as I'm inside it, working my way through, my view of it is partial.

There are ideas of the soul that are well lost, including a great deal that has passed for Christian theology, terrifying or selfishly exalting the individual. The good in what we're working our way to, I feel, is an awareness of all-life, in every creature, in the Earth itself; all the many centres of life, in their otherness, with which we are connected. One result is a new sense of the human body, of human flesh in relation to flesh of the world. But there's also a new sense of spirit – which many now see in nature, but which we shall also have to become aware of in ourselves, in what we are. Can *any* idea of the soul survive the growing consciousness of man and woman as natural beings in the natural world? I don't know. I only know that I can't be appeased by its loss and the implications of its loss, which include connections in the depth with the Creator, and the foundation of personal being. My feeling is that we're beginning, or some people are beginning, late in the day, and possibly too late for our survival, to make amends to nature for the destructive excesses of our unnatural behaviour, behaviour in part justified, it has to be said, by ideas of our spirituality. We are leaning hard, as we have to, towards a sympathetic understanding of nature, and of nature in ourselves, and ourselves in nature. For many people, it seems, the relationship to nature is the new religion. But I don't think this can be finally binding, because there is a flame in us that nature did not ignite, and a need that nature alone cannot satisfy. It may be that we have to cleanse ourselves of false ideas before we can think anew of 'soul' and 'person', and dare to think of 'God'. It may be that our spiritual task is the breaking of images. The remaking of relationships: between humankind and nature, between man and woman, between male and female within the psyche, between one and others. And the breaking of spiritual images that distort these relationships.

Nature, usually, is as far as I can see; but I am aware of other needs.

Later: here, now. A warm afternoon, spring air, blue sky with a fine veil & trails of white cloud.

How wonderful it must be to be a bird singing on a treetop – as I saw an American robin in the cemetery – on such a day!

13 March

Tony has sent me a lovely card, early for my birthday: Jules Léon Montigny, *The wood-cutter*. A man wearing a broad-brimmed hat leans over a felled tree trunk, which he has been cutting. Two horses stand side by side at a short distance from him, harnessed to the sledge on which they will draw the cut wood. From the look of the nearby trees & the sky it's a mild day in winter. In atmosphere the painting reminds me a little of the copy of the B. W. Leader landscape, which Dad made when he was a youth. This too is a moody northern scene, full of solitude. But it's a working world, too – where we come from. 'Thoughts of Pop Mould occurred through this card or without the horses could be myself of course but never had such a splendid hat!'

In the evening, I gave a reading at Le Moyne, in the Firehouse Theatre. It was one of my strongest, including some of the new poems, which I hadn't read in public before, and the people who were there appreciated it. Afterwards, though, I felt a reaction, largely as a result of the people who were not there, including all but three of my colleagues, David & Barbara & Bill Morris, who directs the theatre. It seemed to me so discourteous, so utterly incurious . . . Disillusionment set in, which was alleviated to some extent, as far as Le Moyne is concerned, when I remembered that this was only the same old story of colleagues not attending poetry readings, mine or other poets', familiar to me from all the places at which I have taught, and at most which I have visited. What I find so frustrating is that I *know* I can draw people in to the life of my poems if I can only get them to hear them. This on the same day that I heard from the second literary agent declining to assist me with placing 'Writers in a Landscape'. Yet even as my mood darkened I knew that if a poet can reach only a few people, as I have, it's something to be profoundly grateful for; indeed, a true relationship, that isn't guaranteed by headier reputations. I'm not one who has specialized poetry, but its specialization, in our world of self-obsessed literary coteries, has inevitably affected my ability to find a readership. I've felt for some time that my poetry won't be recognized until after I'm dead, though I realize that it may not be known then either. It would be hypocritical to say that I accept this possibility with equanimity, and don't sometimes rage against it (inwardly or to M.). And untrue to imply that I *need* reputation as an incentive to write, since in writing I find pleasure and meaning: not as an end in itself, but poet is what I am.

15 March
I was a French policeman, outfitted & wearing a peculiar hat, in a film. Mine was a small part and I wasn't quite sure what it was or whether I had to say anything, but it seemed that a road accident was to occur and I was required to be on the spot. So I followed the action around, occasionally meeting real French policemen to whom I explained 'Je suis dans un film', which they accepted – for some reason! – and went on their way smiling. My first girlfriend was playing the main part in the film, which was an emotional one. My part also seemed to involve being at a particular place with two lampposts and a fellow officer, who was short and plump, but somehow we failed to organize things properly in time, and when the film credits were run, I saw with chagrin that I wasn't in it. At the end of the dream, which coincided with the end of the film, I was wretched because my girlfriend ended her relationship with me.

Waking up, and talking with M. about our dreams, I realized that I live *with* the past. Not only *in* it, yet I do live in the past, as M says, in the sense that I relive certain experiences as if I could somehow change them, while she accepts the past as unchangeably past. Yet I live with the past, too; not exactly hoarding it, as my mother and Pop hoarded things, but gathering it in, caring for it, keeping it from oblivion. I share with Dad & Tony & Dave a strong sense of the romance of my existence. J. C. Powys first formulated the idea for me, in his portrait of *his* father, in *Autobiography*, in which I recognized the truth about myself, which seems also to be a family truth. And many of the experiences I dwell with are romantic. I don't have a lover's quarrel with the world, but a lover's relationship.

It isn't only a self-obsession, any more than it was, perhaps, in the case of the Revd. C. F. Powys. It's the people and the places that are real – I love them because they are real, and they are real because I love them. Love doesn't *make* people and places real, which would be unreal if not loved. Love, rather, is our completest form of human knowing. So it isn't only a *self*-romance; it wasn't I who created the people I love, and without them the 'I' I know wouldn't exist. The heart can still be a small, tight thing, wrapped egotistically round a family or a home. But that isn't the truth about me either, though the family & the home may have given me the ground I stand on, and from which I go out to meet and embrace others. It was initially in my parents' love for one another that I came into being. I've lived in that love, too much. And lived to be less idealistic, more sceptical, as I've come to recognize my own imperfect love, and to see in my father, in particular, the selfish face of love. But that's not all; he was a tender and romantic man. I've lived to see more, more sceptically, than I did even when Mother was alive. But I don't doubt that I was grounded on love, which gave me, among other things, a great hunger to reproduce it, in a relationship similar to my parents', or corresponding to my image of their marriage. Much that I have done or sought to do resulted from that.

It's a story I couldn't wholly know, in which vices & virtues, & truth & error, are mixed. It's taken me a long time to know my *difference*, as well as what I have in common with my father and mother, and the knowledge isn't complete. Do I still live *in* the past, to the extent that I'm not really here, now, with M? No. She, more than anyone, has taught me to disentangle myself from the past, to be in the present. But the present is that *now* I write about in *Their Silence a Language*: boy, young man, father . . . It's dwelling with the past, now. Danger lies that way, but so does the truth . . . It's with M that I've learned to become myself, here, now, and with a better understanding of the past. And it's through my children, too, that I've come to recognize differences, theirs from me and from each other, and the absolute necessity of difference to love. That *now* in which the past dwells is the present open to the future – in the boy as well as in the man. We know ourselves the same; we know ourselves other. Neither term can be dispensed with; love needs both.

Another springing day. Green plants pricking up from soil near the house, and yellow crocuses open – wide open – to the sun. Cardinal singing loudly, red against greyish green needles of pitch pine.

Walking up the road, we noticed the different colours of varieties of pine: bluish green, yellow, dark green. Through the gap in the hedge into the cemetery and there, in the grass, were the first daisies, day's eyes fully open. We disturbed four birds, which rose into the air and flew round, piping, sun shining on their white bellies. Returning, we saw them again, on the ground, plovers with black bands round their necks – they must be killdeer, &, maybe, like the curlews at Hafodlas, they come here in the spring to nest. Heat haze over hills beyond the near drumlins.

At first the woods seemed still fast in winter sleep. Then I saw moss which was a richer green, and warm to touch, on the side of two boulders, which I have often walked to this winter – they make a distinct 'place', and I like to think they were a mark for Iroquoian hunters – and found either buried or nearly covered in snow. But today fragments of snow in nearby undergrowth were things that didn't belong. Next we found a few yellow flowers – round faces, consisting of many petals, with a darker yellow sunface at the centre – which had pushed up among dead leaves. I know them from England, their name's on the tip of my tongue.

16 March
Thursday: last classes before the mid-term break. Walked back from college, showered, and went with M for a meal at Korea House on Erie Boulevard. Dusky golden round moon (a day from full) rising beyond the shopping malls along the boulevard, beyond the flat, built-up expanses of the city.

> *When the poet doubts that the center of the universe lies in his own heart, that his spirit is an overflowing fountain, a focus which irradiates creative energy capable of informing and even of deforming the world around him, then the spirit of the poet wanders disoriented again among objects. He doubts their emotive value, and with this lack of esteem for the subject he falls into the fetishism of things. Images no longer attempt to express the poet's intimate feelings, because he himself holds the latter in low esteem, indeed is almost ashamed of them. Images pretend to be trans-subjective, to have the value of things themselves. But if this devaluation of the internal allows the poet any introspection, he will understand that, at the*

> *same time, the world of things has itself been devalued, because it was those very sentiments, already absent or declining, which had imparted all magic to the exterior world.*
>
> Antonio Machado, 'On the Use of Images in the Lyric',
> in Reginald Gibbons, ed., *The Poet's Work*

This is wonderful, but, as it stands, begs questions. What is the heart's ground that it should feel the centre of the universe lies within it? Is it only the poet's internal feelings that give value to the world of things, his sentiments that impart *all* magic to the actual world? Isn't it rather in relationship with that world – in love with the other – that we learn to know and value both it and ourselves? On another occasion, Machado says: 'My feeling . . . is not exclusively mine, but rather *ours*. Without going out of myself, I note that in my feeling other feelings are vibrating as well, and that my heart is always singing in a chorus . . .' He recognizes that he has had to learn language from others, that it is much less *his* than his feelings. 'Before being *ours* – because it will never be *mine* alone – [language] was theirs; it belonged to that world which is neither subjective nor objective, to that third world to which psychology has not yet paid sufficient attention, the world of *other I's*.'

17 March

Evening. We talked about Les[6] – his birthday today, St Patrick's Day.

Is death *always* a blessing (as T. F. Powys maintained), in the sense that life for a desperately sick or incapacitated person would be worse? There is, perhaps, comfort in that, but it's hard to feel.

18 March

A damp, spring morning. I was waiting with two young rabbits, a small girl rabbit and a bigger boy rabbit, at the bottom of Northover Road. At first we were alone, but gradually a crowd of people gathered, waiting for the bus. Sometimes I held one or both rabbits in my arms or on my shoulders, sometimes I set them down on the ground, and watched anxiously in case they went out on the road or were trodden on. They couldn't talk (they *were* rabbits, I *was* me) but we were close to one another and had a good understanding. At last the bus came, the single-

---

[6] Les Arnold, poet and teacher, who died at the age of 49 in 1992.

decker that runs (or used to run) between New Milton and Lymington, and we got on. The driver was sealed off by a glass partition but there was a conductor to whom, with some fiddling in my pockets and wallet to find money, and anxious that I was holding up the other passengers, I paid the fare. Did the rabbits travel free? I'm not sure! Only when the bus was moving down Ramley Road did I realize that the other people hadn't got on. The conductor explained to me that it was the wrong bus; it wasn't going to Lymington, where, presumably, I wanted to go, though no name that I knew was mentioned. I asked him to put us down at the most convenient stop, and to be sure to tell us when we had reached it (for some reason I wasn't hearing him well). He said he would, and we would thus reach our destination before the other people.

The next thing I remember is walking with the rabbits on a track across country, and again the crowd of people is with us. There is something medieval about what happens next: several people on horses, one man (wearing a leather jerkin?) prominent among them, move across the crowd. The horseman takes a liking to the boy rabbit, and wants to have him in exchange for a reddish older female rabbit. I won't let him have my rabbit until the rabbit itself indicates, with a shake of his head, that he wants to go with the man. I walk on, alone again, on a sandy, stony track, and wait for the girl rabbit to catch up with me, and for the reddish rabbit, which is lagging behind. Eventually we come to a ravine with a stream at the bottom of it. I don't know what happens next – except there is another story, in which I have a small part in a play in which Laurence Olivier has the lead, and we are in Westminster Abbey. I am in the pew behind Olivier, with Donald Pleasance, I think, who died recently, and another player with a small part, a young man, has held up proceedings so that we say Olivier should speak to him . . . But this must be another story, for the rabbits, our mutual affection, and my anxiety to protect them, were at the heart of the story that seemed to begin at the bottom of Northover Road, though earlier I had been at Hayford with Mother, and my father had died.

When I woke up and told the dream to M I realized that Emily & Joe were, somehow, *in* the girl and boy rabbits, and my emotion in the dream must have expressed this relation, together with the fact that I thought of the rabbits as girl and boy. But, in the dream, they *were* rabbits, not symbols or human beings transformed into rabbits.

What dreams underline for me, especially dreams that occur in actual places (however transformed), is how closely my identity is bound up with the place-world. Whereas I could now describe the bottom of Northover Road and see it in my mind, in my dream I am *there*. Places live in me more vividly than I can consciously record them. I didn't need to read Edward Casey's book to know that *to be is to be in place*. For the living, this gives the death of loved ones a sharper poignancy. When I think of how real to Mother were the places she knew – the places and the people, especially her father at Park Gate; when I think of her place-world, which she shared with me, to the extent that I saw it, but knew how much more actual it was to her . . . It is enough that death takes from us the people we love (as death will one day 'take' us, whatever that means), but it takes with them their world, the whole, as though pieces of the land break off and float away into the dark. We may know them in our bodies, as we share features with our mother and father, in our disposition, and in what we have learned from them, so that even in deep mind, in imagination & the cave of dreams, their experience becomes our own. But it always remains theirs, and as we receive it so we change it – there is an impassable barrier *between* person and person, there, *within* our common world. Without which, as I have often said, no love – and no loss, no grief.

There are certain feelings, powerful and even all-consuming when felt, that we may later forget we have had, or deny. This is why I want to record, in case I live to disbelieve it, that I once felt I would rather Hayford were destroyed by fire, like a gypsy caravan with all the gypsy's belongings, when he or she dies, than be bought and occupied by other people. I had no arsonist intentions – I was cured of any such thing when I terrified myself by setting a portion of the hedge on fire when, as a boy, I loved to see the sudden flare of dried grass. There was nothing irrational about it; it was simply a powerful feeling. How long ago? Not long; probably as late as when I was living in the Netherlands, before Hayford was sold. It wasn't an early feeling either. I suppose it wouldn't have occurred before my 'possession' of the place became insecure. For *possession* was what it was about: possession and identification. Already the feeling is distant from me; I can understand myself or anyone else having it, but I can't feel it. Letting go is what I've learned to do, and letting be, not wanting to master or possess. Or rather this is what my life is a learning towards. It began, perhaps, when Sue broke the hold I had upon her – made herself free of me, and set me adrift (as it seemed to me then). I remember holding the bowl of our marriage in my hands – an actual physical sensation of holding something that would otherwise fall into pieces. The ability to let go was something I had seen as desirable, to be aimed at, when the children were young, but my entire psychological make-up, during the years at Brynbeidog, was that of a man who couldn't let go, in more than one sense. Positively, it was from Mieke that I learned, by letting myself be loved (strange that that should be difficult, yet longing was always so strong in me, *longing*, not being wholly present), by sexual energy, which holds and exhausts and renews us *now*, and by learning to let my parents die. I have journeyed so far with her that I can now *think* of the man who wanted his original home to be consumed by fire like a gypsy caravan, but I can no longer *feel* with him.

19 March
Sunday morning. A mild air, clouds accumulating in blue sky. White sun of March, shining on silvery grey naked trees. Loud rapping of a woodpecker. Chinking of chickadees. In the woods, we found constellations of coltsfoot – the early flower like a sun – low on the ground beside the path. Glossy green pelts of moss on fallen tree trunks.

> *The civilized nations – Greece, Rome, England – have been sustained by the primitive forests which anciently rotted where they stand. They survive as long as the soil is not exhausted. Alas for human culture! Little is to be expected of a nation, when the vegetable mould is exhausted, and it is compelled to make manure of the bones of its fathers. There the poet sustains himself merely by his own superfluous fat, and the philosopher comes down on his marrow-bones.*
> (Thoreau, 'Walking')

How does Edward Casey get *his* idea of cohabitancy from Thoreau's use of the word in this essay? Thoreau takes Spaulding's Farm as the location of his fantasy of 'some ancient and altogether admirable and shining family,' that had inhabited Nature, not in 'a sort of border life', such as that which he says he lives, but in 'another land'. This is Nature 'on the confines of the actual Concord', but where 'the idea which the word Concord suggests ceases to be suggested'. Thoreau's fantasy is of a family that cohabits with Nature, in a 'house' whose 'coat-of-arms is simply a lichen'. The idea accords with his wish 'to speak a word for Nature, for absolute freedom and wildness, as contrasted with a freedom and culture merely civil'. From Casey's use of the idea I had assumed a way of thinking much closer to Waldo Williams's idea of 'keeping house', in which culture and nature, the generations, and tradition and the living moment, do indeed cohabit. It is a way that would not have abolished the Spauldings and their actual experience, as Thoreau's fanciful vision effectively does.

22 March
Set out on our journey to South Bend, Indiana, driving on Interstate 90 from Syracuse to Ashtabula, Ohio, by Lake Erie. Overnight at the Ronny-Dick motel (named after the owner's sons), from which we set out again on my fifty-fourth birthday.

23 March
Ashtabula to South Bend on long, long roads through flat country. At South Bend we went to the Morris Inn on the campus of Notre Dame University, a quiet, pleasant academic setting after miles of thruway. Late afternoon, John Matthias called for us and showed us round the campus before taking us to his home, where Diana, his wife, prepared us a meal. Afterwards I gave a reading, well attended by students & staff, at the Snite Museum of Art on the campus. My background was an exhibition of paintings by Douglas Kinsey, whom I met in Cambridge during the Poetry Festival, at which M. & I first met. After the reading, during which I'd read from my sequence of Demeter poems, Diana showed us an 18th century French painting, *The Rape of Proserpine*, which depicts another witness to the rape, in Ovid's version: Cyane, the nymph, who, having failed to stop Pluto's chariot and persuade Pluto to 'win' Proserpine rather than force her, merges with the water.

24 March

Frost overnight, the campus lawns white in the morning. After breakfast I talked with James, a postgraduate working on modern war poetry, including David Jones. Later Stephen Fredman, who had also been at my reading, joined us and we talked about Olson and Reznikoff and Jones. Stephen, a warm & responsive man, also gave us directions to Chicago and advice about where to stay.

Later in the morning, under a cloudless sky, we followed his directions and drove to Chicago, passing through the smoke & chemical stink blown across the thruway from Gary and over a bridge surrounded by industrial wasteland into the city.

The relation between Chicago and Gary might be used as a classical illustration of Marx's theory, with the cultural superstructure of Chicago resting on the industrial base of heavily polluted Gary, which one only has to see (and feel in one's eyes & nose & throat) to know that life expectancy must be considerably lower there.

Chicago itself we found visually stunning – soaring, slender skyscrapers, curved roads & waterways, the buildings black and grey and silver and white rising into the blue sky beside the blue waters of Lake Michigan. A place of grace and power, which we saw from our hotel room high above Lakeshore Drive and the Navy Pier, looking out across the lake, and from walking by the river and through the streets.

We found our way by a circuitous route to the Art Institute, where, determined not to repeat the mistake I had made at MOMA, I scarcely glanced at the European work (but couldn't help seeing Brancusi's *Golden Bird* and Chagall's *The Praying Jew*) but went directly to a current exhibition: 'About Place: Recent Art of the Americas'. On this occasion, however, *this* was the mistake, since none of the work had the power of Douglas Kinsey's images, and some of it seemed an excuse for the concepts laid down in the Gallery Guide, instead of being interesting in itself.

What I felt the work of all but two or three of the exhibitors 'lent' was a façade of plausibility to the art-political conventions of the curator.

And that was a shame, especially in Chicago, which is certainly a 'place': elegant & beautiful in its use of modern materials & architectural forms in relation to the natural setting, suggestive of power (power of wealth, power of modern technology), and socially complex, with a mixture of different peoples and of rich and poor. We found it exciting to walk in.

25 March
Chicago sunrise, the sun's molten rim seeming to emerge out of Lake Michigan, and come up and up rising clear of the surface. What awe-inspiring power it must have held for the original natives, without our scientific ideas of cause and effect, without our habit of taking such phenomena for granted – the people who, less than two hundred years ago, and for ages before that, watched beside their lake as the sun rose! And we see it not as a living myth but within our small world of time, measured by the shadows of skyscrapers on the surface of the water. But for all that, I feel the greatness of the city, of this human work that has cost so much to build.

Leaving Chicago early, we passed again by the industrial waterfront, the pylons and plant, through the chemical stink and by smoke that seemed to grow from chimneys, forcing its way into the air. And, under the smoke blowing over, at the end of a tongue of land extending into water, two men had drawn up their truck and were fishing.

On the road again, under a blue sky, traffic well spread out on the long roads, birds of prey sitting in treetops or floating with wings spread over the broad fields of Ohio.

26 March
From Ashtabula to Syracuse on another warm, bright day, azure Lake Erie visible to our left. In New York State, the history compacted into a sentence! 'A main village of the Seneca Indians was at Kanadasaga, now Geneva . . .' The Indian villages were devastated by the Sullivan-Clinton Expedition of 1779, and veterans of the campaign, returning to the area, were granted portions of it 'as a bounty'. They wouldn't have wanted the Indian names, and, instead of creating names suggested by the terrain, they set down the emotional baggage that they had brought with them from the Old World, from Calvin's Geneva. Hence the 'myth of exile', an exile identified with the very places in which they settled, through imported place-names. Or say it was rather an assertion of who they were: not (yet) Americans, but people from Europe, people as good

as any Europeans, with the right to give their places European names. And there, *between* Kanadasaga and Geneva, is the break; a break one is much less aware of in Chicago, because the great city bespeaks white man power (*his* technology, as also in Enrico Fermi's development of the first controlled nuclear chain reaction, despite what it owed to the labour of women & other peoples). But there's more to see in the making of American places than displacement and exile, whether myth or fact. There is emplacement, as in Chicago, with the millions of actual people, many of whom must have found new opportunities. It's the actual that writers and intellectuals often fail to know, because we impose our ideas on experience, both our own and other people's.

31 March
A day of snow; white flakes on the fur of a black squirrel, which came to the verandah looking for food.

2 April
In the cemetery on a fine spring morning. Cardinal singing loudly, excited crows playing in the sky, a pair of killdeer hugging rough ground. I was recently startled to pass a newly dug grave, covered with planks. Now it has been filled in and heaped with flowers. The dead man was 36 years of age. My mind is full of Henry Vaughan. In all honesty, I have to say there's something about his rejection of the world that repels me. His certainty that there is another life, and that it's infinitely more valuable than this. As it repels, so it fascinates: to live completely within such certainty, supported, sustained, the religious language intact. No room for scepticism or doubt. Of course it's myself I know in confessing this, I don't pretend to know Henry Vaughan.

Vaughan's religious certainty – the intactness of his theology and the assurance of his language – is something I can't share, and in which I recognize his strangeness to me. But I was wrong to say his rejection of the *world* repels me. On the contrary, I can sympathize with his re-creation of the divine order as vision, which preserves and protects the Church from the temporary triumph of its enemies. What I can't stomach, in Vaughan or George Herbert, is the rejection of *life*. In effect, though, in rejecting life, they were denying the victory of death. But, surely, one doesn't have to be a modern and a sceptic to feel the gift of life asks more of us.

Vision, in the sense in which I'm using the word here, is far from meaning something vacuous or airy and disembodied; it doesn't refer primarily to Vaughan's cosmic imagery, either. His vision apprehends the divine order, returns to the roots of Christian truth, which he makes visible in image. There's perhaps a sense in which all metaphysical religious poetry is a reaction against the disincarnate word of the Puritans; a poetry written by men who were more or less Catholic in sensibility. Vaughan's religious poetry, written during the Commonwealth, at a time of crisis for the Church of England with its surviving Catholic traditions, responds to the abolition of the Book of Common Prayer, and elevation of the sermon, by *embodying* the old order in vision.

Vaughan's vision fills the universe with the presence of God, and celebrates the promise of a total restoration, in which all beings (including stones) participate. He sounds the psalmist's praises of Creation, and the Welsh praise poet's. His vision is Biblical, centred in Christian theology, but has more than a suggestion of pagan natural sympathy. Yet reaction against the times mustn't be discounted as a shaping influence. In his quiet way, Vaughan is a strong voice of resistance. The things that were banished from his world, from common observance, he stored (and restored) in his poetry. He is a poet of Christian redemption and resurrection, of ultimate restoration in the most inclusive sense – a promise often denied by theologians in their emphasis upon wrath and retribution. His spirit and language (imagery of light, for instance) work both with and against Puritanism, but ultimately more against it, and towards the old faith of the British Church.

Anon is the only poet who is everyman. But when was the last anonymous religious poetry written in English? Before the Reformation, I would think. Vaughan is one of us, not because he is common man, but because of his personal intensity, his affliction, his difference. Rather, he is common because unique. Yet, the thing I must also acknowledge is his strangeness – which inheres in his certainty, his secure foundation upon a religious faith & a religious language, on the far side of the crisis of religious belief and expression in which we live.

5 April
Snow fell heavily yesterday & overnight & it was still snowing in the morning when we set out to drive to New Hartford. There we picked up

Mair and continued on our way to New England. Snow blowing across fields and roads on the way to Utica, but beyond Albany we crossed the snowline.

Strong, cold wind. Woods in the Berkshires smoky grey & purple, whitish, reddish, roadside rock faces tusked with ice, which reminded Mair of stalactites in Cheddar caves.

We reached John & Margaret's home in Florence after lunch, and Margaret took us to visit the Dickinson Homestead in Amherst. Arriving before the guided tour was due to start, we walked in the garden, where a cold wind was blowing across the lawn & flowerbeds, whirling a few dead leaves into the air, chilling the daffodils & purple crocuses. 'It is hard for me to give up the world,' Emily said, when she was a young woman, at a time of religious conversion in Amherst. Easy to see how this place could have been the world for her, a well educated, vividly imaginative woman, who enjoyed close family relationships. The stillness, that sense of this having been *her space*, marked now by her total absence, reminded me of what I'd felt in the Austen home at Chawton, not least because of the relationship between the sisters, Emily & Vinny, Jane & Cassandra. The curator, who gave us a satisfyingly factual, not-too-speculative account of the Dickinson family & of Emily's biography, described her as having had 'a full life'. In the 1860s she experienced 'terror', when her handwriting changed, and she became reclusive, and wrote poems. 'I do not cross my father's ground to any house or town.' Yet here was a world, in the house & gardens, with the well-trodden path to her brother's house; in her mind, which ranged the cosmos. She would have looked out on meadows belonging to the house, where now there are other houses, and on the high ridges of the Berkshires. It would not have been a confined view, as hers was far from being a confined life mentally or spiritually; and as for the married life she did not have, we don't know whether she wanted it, and we do know that many married women were far more imprisoned in narrow circumstances than Emily Dickinson was.

In her bedroom, the thing that fascinated me was a Civil War blanket, red with four dark stripes, which she would kneel on when gardening. The other house in which she lived, on North Pleasant Street, has been demolished, and the site is now occupied by a Mobil Gas Station. It was her room in this house that looked out onto the cemetery, so that as a young woman she would have frequently witnessed burials, and perhaps communed with the dead, or, at any rate, have been daily reminded of death. And that too was integral to her space – the 'distance' between life and death, the journey between house and house, from the world of the living to the narrow room in the ground. As for confinement – women giving birth were confined, Emily Dickinson interiorized cosmic spaces, was labyrinthine in her psychology, and dwelt on that absolute 'distance' which one may know in her space, in the rooms, among the flowerbeds where she once knelt.

In the evening, John drove us into Springfield, where I gave a poetry reading to about a hundred people at the college at which Margaret works. Several people spoke to me warmly & intelligently afterwards, including a young student, a Presbyterian, who told me about his love of nature, and said how much my reading had meant to him.

6 April
Book-buying in Florence and Northampton in the morning. On Margaret's recommendation, I bought a copy of Doug Anderson's poems of the Vietnam War, *The Moon Reflected Fire*, which are very powerful. In one second-hand bookshop, the owner spoke to us about having bought the library of Harvey Swados after his death. Swados, he said, represented a generation of left-wing writers who really did believe their ideas would change the world. They belonged to another age.

In the afternoon Margaret took us first to Smith College, where we visited the Museum of Art. The current exhibition was of Beverly Buchanan's 'Shackworks', sculptures & paintings (vibrant colours, dancing forms), 'inspired by the improvised, handbuilt shelters of migrant and tenant farmers of the Piedmont region of Georgia and the Carolinas': work which would have justified the ideas behind the exhibition we visited in Chicago.

The Smith College Museum of Art has a fine permanent collection. Here I looked at Pierre Bonnard's *Landscape in Normandy*, so rich in colours, with such fullness & depth of nature: a wonderful gathering in. Claude Monet's *The Seine at Bougival*, and a painting of Rouen Cathedral (before he dissolved the built image in light). Jan van Goyen, *View of Rijnland* (1647): tousled grey clouds over flatlands, tiny figures of cattle

& humans, a horizon of houses, windmills, churches, all small in the northern land – and skyscape – grey, green, brown, colours of the Puritan taskmaster north, Puritan and pagan, in which human aspirations make little difference, and the inner weather is as sombre as the clouds. Also some wonderful 19th century American landscapes, reacting against the European tradition: George Innes, *New Jersey Landscape*, Albert Bierstadt, *A Wilderness Lake*, Asher B. Durand (Hudson River Valley School), *Woodland Interior* – a romantic depth the forests of Europe could scarcely rival.

From Smith College Margaret drove us up into the Berkshires – dark blue above us: Mount Holyoke, Sugarloaf, Mount Tom, from which we looked out over Easthampton & towards Amherst & to mountains on the far side, beyond the Connecticut River: dark blue trees & rocks under cloud. Fallen rock stacks among the trees around us, from the precipitous cliffs above. These mountains were visually the limits of Emily Dickinson's world – in fact, a wide expanse, & always suggesting depths of heaven & earth, & depths within the mind.

In the evening we all went to see Margaret & John's son, Brinley, playing the Sheriff of Nottingham in a school musical of Robin Hood. On our journeys in the car Mair often spoke of her beloved brother, Brinley, who died last year. He was a distinguished economist who spent many years working in American universities. Mair has a sister in New Zealand, but other members of her large family remained in Wales. She is an American citizen, but in feeling (and language) she is Welsh. When she felt most homesick for Wales, her husband would advise her to do what he did – work in the garden, put her hands into the soil.

7 April
Having come off the Mass Turnpike onto the 90 in New York State, and into the 55 mph speed limit zone, we were stopped by the police and given a ticket for speeding; another addition to our American experience.

At a roadside service area I studied a fascinating exhibit: 'Modern Route, Ancient Roots': the Hudson-Mohawk Transportation Corridor from Hunting Trail to Superhighway. Mohawk 3112: 'Today, thundering through ancient valleys where Mohawk braves once fought, their modern "Mohawks" too are on the warpath' (from a N. Y. Central Railroad ad., 1944, which depicts trains speeding 'the Victory traffic' (and doesn't, of course, mention whom the 'braves once fought'). Governor Dewey, opening the New York Thruway on June 24, 1954, described it as the 'Erie Canal of the Atomic Age'. A journalist writing in a lead article, October 1959: 'It stretches from Niagara to New York City, from a great lake to a great ocean. And it is greater than the Falls, the lake, the ocean, or even the metropolis.

For it is a magical road – in concept, in construction, in public service. It is the New York Thruway'.

Under the road the ancient routes; but in what sense can they be described as roots?

Imagine a man in the ditch,
The wheels of the overturned wreck
Still spinning –

I don't mean he despairs, I mean if he does not
He sees in the manner of poetry
    (George Oppen, from 'Route')

Awe-inspiring, though: the will, the effort of men. With imagination, we may feel the pull of the mud track in the photograph of farmers travelling by horse & cart to market before the turn of the century; or see the narrow concrete road under the wheels of the first cars. How rapidly we have cut down through the earth – Erie Canal, obsolete in less than a century; railway; superhighway. And some of us trail after with our minds, or try to stand in one place, saying that the billion flashing journeys don't alter the meeting with earth & heavens & gods. And perhaps they don't; but we have also created a world which most of us can't imagine.

14 April
I learned earlier in the week that Glyn Jones has died. Later I talked about Glyn with Tony Curtis, after he had given a poetry reading at Le Moyne. All of us who had known him said the same thing: Glyn was a Christian gentleman.

    He would have smiled at such a portentous description. But Glyn was truly a gentle, kind & courteous man, considerate of other people, and self-contained, in command of himself. He was based firmly on a loving knowledge of the people he came from, on the individuals & their values, on their society. Like Roland Mathias, he knew what he owed to his people, and he acknowledged his own shortcomings accordingly, but without Roland's puritanical self-lacerating. Glyn felt the appeal of romantic revolt, but he refused the way of the bourgeois artist, unlike his friend Dylan Thomas.

I now think this is why I made him angry when we first met, at Gregynog: because I showed self-pity, revealing something of the anguish (I called it 'terror') that I felt at that time. Glyn was concerned for me, as a man and a writer, because I was letting out inner experience.

The spirit in which he wrote honours his people; he helped to create an alternative tradition to that of the writer as bourgeois rentier. Welsh writers in English have been able to make themselves at home in Wales – in more than one sense – because of Glyn.

Easter
Daffodils, taking the winds of April. First dandelions in the grass of the cemetery.

A name and date caught my eye:

EDWARD D FORGETTE
NEW YORK
CPL BTRY F 60 FIELD ARTY
WORLD WAR 1
March 23 1897   Feb 10 1964

Under the cross in a circle, inscribed on a flat stone.

On Saturday evening we went with Terrie to the Easter Vigil – Night-Watch of the Resurrection at Holy Cross Church, DeWitt. I was moved by the symbolism of the lighted candles, by the sense of community in the packed church, with children's voices punctuating the readings & singing, which also moved me – with the exception of some savage Old Testament passages. I was held, hushed; not only because it brought back the past. And still I stand outside, torn between seeing it all as a poetic story, that brings people together, and feeling the enormous miracle of the claim . . . Yet withal not agonized, nor thinking of myself above it all. In the heart and mind of the believer knowledge belongs to God. He alone knows.

Over the weekend I wrote my essay on Henry Vaughan.

It seems to me there's little enough time to know anything by oneself. It isn't with idle curiosity that I read the names & dates on gravestones, or out of morbidity. Always I think of the life, a completed life – and thus of what substance my own has.

Especially in the Catholic cemetery, where there are many family graves, I think of the life that is lived with and among others, alone, yet also sustained, supported, lived with love. If the thought of death makes me solemn, it also makes me realize that I'm not serious enough – that I don't always know the ground I stand on – am often frivolous, in a way my poems are not. Yet I don't make a religion of poetry; rather poetry seems to me to be serious when it is religious: seeking reality, asking & being asked ultimate questions, & wondering, walking in joy, for to be serious isn't to be heavy, humourless, joyless.

If I'm religious it's because I don't make a religion of poetry – though it is my true way of knowing, and in a sense I live by & for it, because it's the voice of my being. Yet it speaks of what is beyond me, is open to the reality I don't construct, the reality beyond words.

I've thought of ground as what I write *from*. But it would perhaps be truer to say ground is what I seek to open to, as a channel communicating with the life I did not invent.

Thinking of an acquaintance's broken marriage and remembering my own first marriage, I remember an old photograph from the Children's Encyclopedia I had when I was a boy – it was already old, out-dated long before my birth. In the picture in my mind, two horses are pulling against each other. They are fastened by chains to an iron ball, which is between them, and they strain against it. I can't remember why, and perhaps never knew. But there is the image: two horses in iron chains, straining against each other. Of course, some people have been held together against their wills, bound by a loveless and even mutually destructive marriage. Thomas Hardy knew about that: he felt it was *the* theme of his time. And how, I wonder, would he have regarded the freedom we have achieved. There are relationships that have to be broken. And there's the dream (not always a dream) of bonds that hold, which I and many others grew up with.

I could be moved to write an 'Ad Posteros', because I like Henry Vaughan's, and the idea appeals to me. But there's nowhere I could stand to look down on the times in which I live.

19 April
First white anemones in the woods: windflowers, on a windy day in April.

The butterfly driven by the wind has more direction than the flying leaf.

23 April
At the Rome Art & Community Center, where we heard Margaret give a good reading of her poems – some of them set in Aberystwyth, which doesn't seem a world away when we are with members of the Lloyd family. David went with us, and we met Richard and Louise and Mair, as well as Margaret, at the Center, and had a meal with them afterwards, at a Greek restaurant near New Hartford.

The Center is housed in what is largely a mock Jacobean building – it reminded us of a smaller Gregynog – so convincing I thought it might have been brought over brick by brick, but this wasn't the case. The wife of an industrialist designed it, and it was built in 1923. Her specification was: 'I want a house that Jane Austen would have wanted to live in'. A 'world famous art collector' furnished the interior. 'The local community was witness that summer to a parade of trucks bringing priceless court cupboards, 17th century chairs, wall hangings, floor coverings and other antique furnishings and art treasures from New York.' Mock or not, the house has a pleasant, antique atmosphere.

After the reading, we drove back as the light was fading, on Genesee Street, once the Red Indian track, on a ridge with far views over the Mohawk Valley. Spacious upstate New York! Much as I'm looking forward to going home to England, I shall miss these spaces, & the sense of possibility that they awake in the mind.

25 April
Welcome Chloe Jacqueline, our grandchild, born 4.16 p.m. today, at Winchester Hospital! I was in class when Joe rang to tell Mieke. In the evening (1 a.m. for him, in a phone box at Middle Wallop), he rang again

to talk to me. It was a quick birth, but Maddy had to have stitches. Joe was full of praise for her, for her strength & power of endurance & uncomplaining, for her & for women's possession of these qualities. He spoke with great tenderness and wonder of his little daughter, of how he held her, and she turned from purple to pink in his arms, and opened her eyes – this, in particular, the child opening her eyes for the first time!

Chloe was born with a mass of black hair. Just as Joe was. Not so long ago, it seems to me! And of course I live it again, or certain things that I remember. From his birth, from the time when he was a little boy. Here, M. & I opened a bottle of champagne and toasted Chloe and her mother and father.

29 April

Morning: a pair of American goldfinches, the male bright yellow & black, in the hazel by the verandah.

Alternating bright sun & cloud shadow, warmth in sheltered places, strong wind. I saw a woodpecker – a common flicker – in the woods, one of a family that flew up as I approached. This one settled on a branch and swayed with it in the wind, grey on grey except for the bird's red nape. White & purple violets. Yellow lilies (adder's-tongue?), hanging heads, mottled pointed leaves, growing against tree trunks. Grassy areas of the cemetery a mass of dandelions, where, recently, there were only a few. Birds with loud voices – American robins, cardinals – singing to their own purposes in the woods & from trees in the open, but as though they would whistle up the grass & flowers, the plants pushing aside layers of dead leaves.

Reading Lev Shestov again: if one founds one's thought on God, with whom all things are possible, it's easy to make a mockery of reason & to scorn all human thought. For a poet, that may be the best way – to root oneself in wonder, which no form of words can ever satisfy. But, if there is no God? If there is only for each being this living moment, & the ever-changing skies of memory that illuminate now one moment, now another, flashing light, spreading darkness? How can anyone be so sure there is a God? Faith. Jung said he *knew*. (But I don't trust Jung.) Pascal. Shestov. Not the God of the philosophers. But suppose the atheists are right. That is what I *suppose*, but am not certain of. And it casts the responsibility upon us to make meaning – and love is meaning, given between people, and wonder, and the pleasure that there is in life itself. These are meaning, even if we die into nothingness. And if we don't have them while we are alive we will have nothing. I don't want any God-fearing thinker to tell me this life doesn't matter, or is a preparation for another and better one. If I don't find meaning in the moment I don't live. And to find is to bring as well as to receive.

The absolute freedom Shestov and Berdyaev speak of means nothing to me. I want to be free to watch a bird or to kneel on the earth to look at a flower, and bird and flower exist, I am free to respond to them, to gain an enlarged sense of their being. My freedom is not to invent from nothing, but to relate to the other; and indeed that is what sets me free. I don't even understand the idea of absolute freedom. I would have thought that what matters most for a Christian is to love Christ, to love God in Christ, to love our fellow beings in Christ. What then is absolute freedom for? Isn't it enough to love the person, the unique being, to open in love towards the reality of the other? Isn't that knowledge in love the closest we can come to an absolute? What can we want except to be in relationship, to another, to God? Is it possible that thinkers such as Shestov and Berdyaev want more than love? And can what is more than love be other than some vanity of thought? How easy it is to miss the real. This is a dreamworld, we are asleep most of the time, I agree entirely with Shestov about that. But my idea of the real is more literal – it is the flower, the bird, the person: each being and the world we share with them, which we can wake into only through love, and in which all thought that takes us away from that is part of the dream. Insofar as I dare to formulate any idea of God, He is lover and knower of the real, with a love the blessed may feel, and a knowledge we can only wonder at, that is infinitely beyond us.

7 May
Chloe, a young herb, a green shoot. And here the leaves are unfolding on trees & shrubs, small green & red claws on the hazel by the verandah, yellowy-green leaves like flowers on maples. The woods are touched with green; in the midst, a tall, charcoal-black cherry, white blossom high up among the treetops. Over the bank beside the house, now a mass of periwinkles and grass, where a big rabbit often sits at evening,

contemplatively chewing, we can still see out to the hills of upstate New York, over the Jamesville limestone quarries, hidden from us, but marked by red lights. But soon all this will be concealed by foliage, which will come all in a rush now that the days are warmer and getting hot.

I finished my marking yesterday. I shall miss the Le Moyne students, especially the group in my Advanced Poetry Workshop. It has been a privilege to be their teacher. Some, working through confusion. Most, making discoveries, in some cases with a combination of keen intelligence and a kind of innocence that is moving and refreshing. Jon Bissell, who gave me a wonderful ink drawing of a bear, wrote: 'America! That's about as big and tumultuous a subject as anyone could hope for'. I've had no doubts about being a teacher this year. I haven't needed to: teaching courses I enjoy, with students I like, two days a week! No administration! But I don't think I've ever regretted being a teacher anyway. The problems I've had have been with academicism. I've been drained of energy periodically, and experienced conflict between the need to write and the obligation to teach, drawing on the one source of energy and time.

Solipsism has been one of my great temptations; is a perennial danger. And what it leads to is Hell. It's knowledge of others that saves me from it; in their self-disclosure that I witness as a teacher, for example. It's a simple enough thing that I'm saying; but in our time, with the foundations of the common world shattered, the hardest thing for the mind to know. *For the mind*, because thought leads us away from one another, into the desert.

The contempt of the intelligentsia for others, for those they regard as *Das Man*, or 'bourgeois', and for all representatives of the Establishment or status quo, pervades the century. In the 60s I assumed it as a kind of virtue. Later I began to find my way back. Now I wonder whether in the coming century, the next millennium, we will learn to think towards one another again. It isn't a matter of fellow feeling alone, but of altering a mind-set: opening it to the spaces between us, to the Earth and its places. For as long as we manipulate others with ideas we distance ourselves from our kind. I have scarcely been tempted to identify criticism – literary criticism – with overstanding writer or text, or with fault-finding. But I have had to find my way back – I am finding my way back – from an assumed superiority, based on 'intelligence', to recognize its stupidity, not only its heartlessness, but the ideology of the closed mind. I have seen greater understanding in others, without my intellect. I have questioned what intelligence is, and what it is for. As a teacher, I have met personal and intellectual qualities that have knocked me off my conceit.

Intellectual hatred justifies anything: the bomb in Oklahoma City, genocide. It is the mind that we forge into a weapon of hatred. It isn't easy to disarm oneself.

8 May
Fiftieth anniversary of VE Day. I remember the long trestle tables in the lane outside Fairacre, the crowd of neighbours (but I can't *see* a single face, not even my father's or mother's on that occasion), and, at night, fireworks, highflung *green* stars. I think it was then that I was told we were celebrating Victory.

9 May
After dark, rain and a noise outside – a distant phone buzzing? – which we recognize as a cicada, the first to break the long silence since late in the fall.

12 May
Moist grey days, moist new leaves. Bird with red triangle on his breast & heavy beak – a rose-breasted grosbeak – among pink & white blossom on a bush near the house.

13 May
At Stone Quarry Hill Art Park. The visit began with a sighting of another bird that was new to us – a northern oriole fluting from a treetop. Later we saw swallows, and, as we drove away, glimpsed what may have been a tanager – a bird of several bright colours, as though it had been dipped in a paint pot

The object of our visit was an exhibition, and especially a work on which Kim had collaborated with the poet, Pat Lawler, whom we met for the first time. They were both uncertain about it, and Kim felt it misrepresented her. But we liked it, and felt it more arresting than most of the other works on show. Other things included earth and stone sculptures by Tom Huff, a Native American artist, who had also brought some of his small, soapstone carvings, one of which we bought.

The ethnic mixture of artists suggested a certain political correctness in the choice of exhibitors. In the panel discussion a black sculptor talked about the political anger that informed his work; but no one could have guessed it from the pieces themselves, which had a kind of conventional formalism.

The art world in the States is highly sensitized to ethnic & racial issues. It's a complex situation: justice certainly requires that artists from among the different peoples should have equal opportunities, and it's by no means the case, of course, that the only important artists are white males! But it is true also that *political* choices lead to the privileging of some poor art, both in terms of what is shown and as an influence on what is made. Reading poems and looking at works of art produced in America today I'm depressed by the programmatic quality of a lot of the work – the sameness of complaint, for example. There are striking exceptions, of course – in individual vision and in use of alternative traditions. But these are in danger of being swamped by an art and writing of conventional gestures.

How to reconcile a belief in the need to encourage everyone to explore their artistic potential – a need we fall far short of fulfilling – with the necessity of artistic values, and therefore of critical judgment? Here and there an individual succeeds in reconciling the needs; but as a culture we're hopelessly mired in the contradictions, not least because it has become an academic convention to deny the existence of values.

Will poetry and art survive into the next century? Some people say they are dead already. They're not, of course. But sometimes I think only the dead thrive – the imitative, the empty, the fashionable. The creative mind struggles, its work obscured by the ersatz, cut off from those who would receive it. In one direction or the other – democracy/individual artistic excellence – thought stops. We want one or the other; we don't see how we can have both. Yet what do we need more than to know our common humanity, which is for each a source of creative possibility? And it is human to admire, to compare, to discriminate.

16 May

Late afternoon. Buttercups, bright yellow, in the grass of the cemetery, white wild strawberry flowers, butterflies. As I step through a gap in the hedge my spirit lifts with the opening view – wide blue sky, line of the far Adirondacks. Ironically I've tired the eyes of my mind by reading David Jones intensively, my first complete re-reading in years.

As I climb the hill a crow sees me from a distance and flies off cawing alarm to its mate. There are many dandelion clocks where the crows were, in unmown grass alongside the woods.

The woods are no longer stark now, but magical with the play of light & moving leaves. *Weet, weet, weet, weet, weet* – a cardinal, black-bearded, bright red, whistles loudly from a treetop, among soft, green leaves.

I begin to walk off my heaviness, thinking, watching.

I sent the typescript of *Our Lady of Europe* to Stephen this morning.

17 May

Richard & Louise, Barbara & Jack, & David joined us over wine & food in the afternoon, & Sean & Suzanne came in later. Their company helped to relax me – the day was sultry and I've been feeling under pressure recently. In the evening we drove to Cazenovia, where I gave a reading at the college, which Kim organized. As well as students from Cazenovia, a number of friends, including Roger Lund & Pat Keene, came over from Syracuse. I was grateful to them for coming, and although I didn't feel like reading, it went well, and I showed slides of Lee's sculptures too. Afterwards we had a meal & drinks in a bar in the village.

18 May

After another morning of work, as I went out with M., I suddenly realized why I'm feeling under pressure. It isn't only because of the reading, which I've been doing intensively since the end of term. It's because in my attention to David Jones's writing & thought, in my fidelity, my determination not to misread or misrepresent, I've lent my mind to his work, and given up my creative freedom. There's also perhaps something in the nature of the demands his beliefs make, & in the Old World material, that takes me back into the past – not only into history & myth, but into my past, when I've followed his mind. The reading is immensely rewarding; at times, in rereading *In Parenthesis*, for example, the work delights & moves me. Yet I'm oppressed by the closeness with which I follow his 'meanders', the sense of responsibility I bring to 'getting it right'.

And when I have done the work, what will I know that I didn't know twenty years ago, when I prepared a lecture on a similar theme, for the conference Roland Mathias organized in Aberystwyth? *Something*: more detail, possibly more knowledge in depth, together with a keener sense of the complexity of the subject. But perhaps nothing really new.

I have the lecture to write, and the programme about David Jones to make for the BBC when we return to England. But perhaps what I most need to do, for myself, is write the elegy, which I've been postponing since the time of his death. A commemoration & celebration, which speaks of him faithfully – but in my way, in my words & images; mine in the sense that they're of the things that have made me. It may be more difficult than it was, in the event, to write 'Variations on a Theme by Waldo Williams' because I know so much more about David Jones than I do about Waldo Williams. Knowing more one is less free to invent, to imagine. Perhaps that is so. David Jones probably wouldn't have agreed; for him, making paintings & poems meant gathering all in, losing nothing of the *material*. But what I have to recognize is the differences between us – differences that make me uneasy when I think of myself as a moralist, instead of as a sign-maker, one who holds up bodily images. For it's in his sacramentalism, his placing of himself in the order of signs, that he powerfully attracts me. In his making of 'things', which have no taint of self-expression.

There's nothing of the search for meaning in his work. He starts from meaning – the quest is for contemporary signs of what he apprehends as eternally real.

But that's not where I start.

Love chose him; like Eric Gill, he fell in love with the truth. The devotional element in David Jones's work is plain to see; the love informing his recalling of 'sweet Mair' & the *geong haeled thaet waes God Almihtig*, in the words of *The Dream of the Rood*. He was such a man as the Anglo-Saxon who wrote that poem; and he was closer to the medieval Langland than to almost any later poet except Gerard Manley Hopkins.

It's the Catholicism that I draw back from: the obedience, & the sacerdotalism. From that, and because I am drawn *to* another history, another *common* reality. And because there's something in me that sympathizes with the image-breakers . . . I don't want to be a moralist, or a man endlessly speculating. I too want to be able to hold up the things I love, and, like Aneirin, to honour the men (& women) of valour. But I don't belong to the Church, and I don't regret that I'm not part of a culture. I don't turn in despair from the modern world – in effect, from post-medieval Europe. There are other 'deep things' belonging to the Island, another England, another Wales.

I will try not to simplify or falsify David Jones. But when I write as a poet about him, with love, it must be from my things that I shape the song.

19 May

It is the *humanity* that I love in David Jones's art: a humanity that expresses human being and is manifested in friendship, in creatureliness – not just 'love of nature', but kinship with earth, animals, trees – a bond with all *in the flesh* – and in care for the living and the dead, in gratitude, in making. There is a unity in his work that stems from this quality. It's present in the trenches of *In Parenthesis*, for example, and also in his representation of animals and landscapes. It has diverse manifestations, in writings & paintings with or without human figures, but all of which embody the quality of his feeling.

This is what I've responded to in David Jones from the beginning: something that's more than the 'I feel' of romantic subjectivity; feeling embodied in rhythm, shape in words, image, verbal & visual 'thing'. And in subject: the things of the Island, from the geological making & movements of peoples & cultural formations. Not the only England, the only Wales, but a deeper Britain, known & loved, than that of most other twentieth-century artists & writers.

It seems to me now that in his ideas about culture & man the artist he sought an impossible *conceptual* unity. And I feel there's a consequent narrowing in his vision, in his focus on the Island as part of Catholic Europe. In a way, he never accepted the Reformation, or even Britain after 1282, when, with the death of Llewelyn, the 'last' Prince of Wales, the connection with the unity formed under the Romans was severed. 'Denied the vision of hope he could only see what lay behind – the smouldering ruins of man's history and a litter of broken things.' So wrote Philip Hagreen about David Jones after Petra Gill had broken off their engagement. And there's *some* truth in it, I think, though it wasn't necessarily the broken engagement that caused the denial. Or say there's a logic, given his religious beliefs, in his denial of the post-Reformation world, of all that is not sacramental . . . What I feel, in part as a result of frustration born of trying to follow his thought, is that he sought an impossible conceptual unity, and that while his feeling gathers all in, at the level of idea, his vision fragments.

It's at this point, though, that I have to recognize the difference of our backgrounds, not just the fact that I don't share his dogma – though that's crucial – but that I was brought up in a different time, and another social world. So that it isn't only an intellectual difference that separates us, but, in some instances, a love of different things. And as I immerse myself in his world, intent on not misreading or misrepresenting it, so it is my things, & the creative freedom I enjoy by virtue of being the person I am, that I lose touch with.

26 May
Looking back on the week, indeed, on most of the month since the semester ended, I find that I've done little except work on my paper for the Conference on Welsh Studies. Yesterday evening, though, we spent with Jack & Barbara at her house on Lorraine Avenue, a small house by American standards, which, with the trees around, and the painted walls and old paintings and books inside, has such a restful, 'green' atmosphere. It seemed to me like a sacred space, which pleased Barbara, who has remade her life since living here, and written many poems. She and Jack are wonderful people, creative & intelligent, thinking for themselves, expressing themselves individually. They have the humanity which, I realize more & more, is the life of art & thought, and without which academia, the world of the 'arts', philosophy, religion, simply die.

Today we made an excursion with our dear friends Kim & David, or rather they took us out. First, on a lovely cloudy leafy morning (Memorial Day, small flags waving on veterans' graves), they took us to Skaneateles, where, near the beautiful lake, we had lunch in the restaurant Terrie had taken us to, at the beginning of our visit to the States.

After lunch, we went to the Montezuma wetlands nature reserve.

Here, over long grasses ruffled by a breeze, we watched Canada geese & goslings on ponds, & swallows, brilliant electric-blue swallows, flying round & perching on their nest-boxes, where little faces looked out of the holes. We looked at an osprey's nest in a tree in the middle of marshland. The others saw the birds, but I couldn't convince myself that I did. We looked too at an eagle's nest in a similar situation. Best of all, we saw herons, a small one, and several great blue herons, standing in water bending & unbending their long supple necks, looking utterly primeval; and six turtles sunning themselves on a log that projected over the water, sun shining on their shells. Red-winged blackbirds perched on rushes here & there.

We then drove on roads alongside Cayuga Lake to Ithaca, where we visited the Herbert F. Johnson Museum of Art on the campus of Cornell University. From the top of this new building one looks down over woods & the town at a long, blue stretch of Cayuga Lake – one of the marks made by God's fingers when he blessed the earth, according to the Red Indians. The thing that really arrested me in the Museum was Giacometti's *Walking Man Two*. A tall, emaciated figure with a texture of crumbling bronze, one might see it, in Sartrean terms, as a figure secreting emptiness, or reduced almost to nothing under the great weight of alien space. But to me it appeared heroic, and it dominated the room with its presence, where it stood in the middle, in mid-stride.

In the next room I was struck with equal force by another work, though for different reasons. This was Constable's painting of Netley Abbey, so unexpected there, or anywhere, since I didn't know he had made a painting of the Abbey – the ruins by Southampton Water, which I know well. It's an oil painting strong in atmosphere. The stone of the ruin glimmers white, surrounded by dark trees, and under a stormy sky in which crows are being buffeted by the wind. On one side, stands a dark red figure, which is distinguished from, yet part of the sombre, violent scene: surprisingly violent for a ruined abbey, but in which the forces of nature rage unobstructed, where once religious order prevailed and the sweet birds sang.

30 May
Set out on a cloudy morning to drive to Columbus, taking another route from the one we had taken to Notre Dame. At first through damp

green wooded hills, by the glacial lakes at Tully, to Cortland and on to Binghamton. Towards Scranton the carnage of deer on the roads began, which we saw over a wide area, both coming and going, with dead animals lying beside the highways, and sometimes reduced to a barely recognizable mess on the road itself. Deer were the most conspicuous, but there were raccoons & woodchuck & other species as well. And the traffic speeds on, as, usually, it has to, if human carnage isn't to be added to the rest.

At Harrisburg we crossed the broad Susquehanna River, & after a day of driving over & through mountains, stopped for the night at a hotel in Somerset, a former mining town in the Alleghenies. Earlier, on banks by roadsides above the Ohio River, we saw the first dog roses.

31 May
From Somerset to Columbus, where, in their house in a pleasant suburban road in Arlington, we visited Dick & Afkham Davis. Their daughter Mariam, whom I met when she was a little girl (she didn't like my beard), is thirteen now, and her sister, Mehri, is ten. In the evening we went to hear Mariam playing the violin with a group of fellow pupil musicians on a small circular stone stage in a park beside a river; and lay on the grass with Dick & Afkham, among other parents, enjoying the music & the sunlight through leaves.

Last time I saw Dick, in Aylsham, he scarcely knew where the next cheque was coming from, and was worried for the sake of his wife & daughter. Now he's a respected, even renowned, Persianist with a professorship at Ohio State University. He feels no strong sense of belonging to Columbus or the States, though Mariam & Mehri do, but is friendly with a number of colleagues in his department. He says that, through his studies & translations, he lives a good deal in the Middle Ages. When we talked about our mutual friend Lindsay Clarke (whom Dick calls Vic), he shows that's he almost as pessimistic as Lindsay about the future. Dick has a particular sense of the West's mistake in making an enemy of Islam, and he believes that modern communications will, by revealing to the poor of the world the great disparity between their living standards and those of the well-off, lead to an apocalyptic outcome. He feels completely cut off from contemporary poetry in England, and has few connections with poets in the States.

My sense of connection to England is much closer than Dick's. Yet we've more in common than I could once have acknowledged. I remember that, seeing him in Aylsham among his neighbours, I felt he had what I wanted: to belong to a community. In the meantime I've come to realize how tenuous my belonging actually is, and to think about it more realistically.

1 June
Leaving Columbus early in the morning, we drove, at first in fog and rain, south to the University of Rio Grande, Ohio, where we attended the First North American Conference on Welsh Studies. Grand names both, for a small college, and a conference that was, in fact, well attended, with some distinguished speakers. Here we met old friends, Walford & Hazel Davies, & Ned Thomas, as well as David (who had flown into Columbus from Syracuse), and several other people with whom we got on well, including Patrick Ford from Harvard, and David Klausner, with whom I talked about T. F. Powys. John Davies, the historian, gave the keynote address. Ned Thomas's talk characteristically covered a wide field: minority cultures, romantic ideas of cultural identity contrasted with the actuality of Welsh or Basque or Catalan experience, Matthew Arnold & the Celtic Twilight, and Waldo Williams's wonderful poem 'Mewn Dau Gau'. Equally characteristically, I perked up when he quoted something I'd said, and from then on felt more involved in the conference. Late in the afternoon, I shared a reading with David, and read poems from 'Under Mynydd Bach' and 'Variations on a Theme by Waldo Williams'.

2 June
The second day of the conference began with a persuasive &, as usual, gracefully delivered lecture by Walford on 'Fern Hill', which made me want to rethink some of my prejudices against Dylan Thomas. In particular, Walford's emphasis on Dylan Thomas's need to recapture the integrity of the child's vision helped me to realize the impact of the war on Thomas. Above all, though, Walford is a sensitive & intelligent *reader*, who illuminates the poet's use of language.

In the afternoon I gave my lecture on David Jones, in which I said things that matter – but the more I say on the subject, the more I see there is to say. It went well, and I probably said as much as I could in an hour, but it left me with a view of the gaps.

3 June
A long day's drive. As we neared Williamsport, the first thunderstorm stopped us, and battered the car with hailstones. We drove on when it had passed but were close to storms most of the way, violet forked lightning flashing to ground in the hills. Between Elmira and Ithaca rain flooded down again. Back in Syracuse at last, the air was clear and sweet.

4 June
A summer morning stroll in the cemetery. A killdeer running from me, flying a short distance, running again, trying to distract me from chicks that must have been close by. In the woods, I sat on one of the two boulders that I've often visited during the winter and spring. A chipmunk came quite close to me, then suddenly ran away very fast, running and jumping through the air, and went behind a tree, squeaking. Walking and sitting down I had felt at peace. Now I realized what fearsome beings we are to other creatures. It's what one knows, of course, but rarely feels.

For the religious there's an ultimate belonging beyond anything that can be obtained on earth. What I feel as I travel farther from childhood & adolescence, & from the belief that I would somehow go *back*, is a greater ability to share things with other people, some or all of whom 'belong' no more than I do. With old friends, for example, I feel I am more *there* than I once was, when my mind was set on the impossible return. And with strangers. It also becomes possible to recognize where one does belong – to relationships, to a small group of people, perhaps to an interest or an institution. But I'm only saying what I thought I'd learned from Martin Buber, all those years ago when I was afraid to leave home and go down to Aberystwyth to meet people. Over & over again the need to find the place that lies between – the place that opens to the ground.

Evening. Meal with David & Kim in an excellent Thai restaurant in Armory Square, Syracuse. Afterwards we walked in the city center under a quarter moon.

5-6 June

A last morning of packing & a final visit to Le Moyne. Champagne with Terrie, & with David & Kim, who then drove us with all our bags to the airport for our flight to Boston.

At night, on the plane, barely the dark red ember of sunset then the first faint upspreading blue of dawn over the Atlantic. During a cramped, sleepless night I read, looked out over the wing at sky, and watched a programme about the internet & cyberspace. The people interviewed talked about the creation of a new kind of human being, a new form of community, in which individuals equipped with the latest technology communicate with one another across all barriers & frontiers, negating all old ideas of society & social authority. The programme maker was pessimistic, depicting a technological paradise for a few who are able to abandon the reality in which the rest of us live.

Arriving exhausted at Gatwick, & after a long time waiting in a crowd to retrieve our luggage, we were met by Joe & Emily, and Joe drove us to Middle Wallop, where, in their cosy home in the converted fire lorry, parked with the vehicles of a few fellow travellers along a drove under trees, we saw Maddy & little Chloe, all sleepy & black-haired, a lovely little girl. Joe then drove us on to Frome, left the hire car for us to use, and took the train back to Salisbury. He couldn't have done more to ease our return for us.

At first everything was strange – the side of the road we were driving on, the intimacy of the green countryside, the money, ways of talking & the usually less friendly casualness. Strangest of all the familiar, as we passed Cley Hill and came home. What causes the strangeness is the double perspective: here & not here. I'm still in the house in Syracuse, in the rooms, or on the local roads, and at the same time I'm here, in this different place, which I know with an old intimacy that has yet to re-establish itself. And tiredness adds to an almost hallucinatory feeling; our feet aren't quite touching the ground.

www.ingramcontent.com/pod-product-compliance
Lightning Source LLC
Chambersburg PA
CBHW031150160426
43193CB00008B/323